California Mediterranean

California Mediterranean

Photography by Melba Levick
Text by Marc Appleton

RIZZOLI
NEW YORK

First published in the United States of America
in 2007 by
RIZZOLI INTERNATIONAL PUBLICATIONS, INC.
300 Park Avenue South, New York, NY 10010
www.rizzoliusa.com

ISBN-10: 0-8478-2915-4
ISBN-13: 978-0-8478-2915-6
LCCN: 2006935716

Designed by Abigail Sturges

Printed and bound in China

2007 2008 2009 2010 2011/ 10 9 8 7 6 5 4 3 2 1

FRONT COVER *Arcady Pavilion and its grand garden stair against the mountains. The eucalyptus trees, Champagne fountain, and covered stone are all original to the estate (p. 176).*

BACK COVER *Stained glass window in Casa Nueva (p. 130).*

PAGE 1 *Gladding McBean pots on the patio, Casa de las Campanas (p. 186).*

PREVIOUS PAGES *View from Casa Leon of the Pacific Ocean over stone statues from Florence, Italy (p. 98).*

CONTENTS

INTRODUCTION

FIG. 1

PREVIOUS PAGES *View of Montalba from the boxwood parterre with carved Italian basin and checkerboard wall of Mexican brick and leftover Italian limestone (p. 26).*

FIG. 1 *Mission San Luis Rey de Francia, California, 1798. Image originally published in Rexford Newcomb's* The Old Mission Churches and Historic Houses of California *(Philadelphia: J. B. Lippincott Co., 1925), p. 106.*

FIG. 2 *Glenwood Mission Inn, Riverside, California, 1902. Image originally published in Rexford Newcomb's* The Old Mission Churches and Historic Houses of California *(Philadelphia: J. B. Lippincott Co., 1925), p. 356.*

In common references to California architecture, the terms Mediterranean, Spanish Colonial, and Mission styles have often been used interchangeably. This has been especially true with regard to the period in Southern California's architectural history beginning roughly at the end of the nineteenth century and extending to the 1930s when these styles were first prominent. To complicate matters, the chronology of each of the styles overlapped, and they were not necessarily mutually exclusive. As the growth of building in Southern California increased, elements from one were often adapted to another. This was not surprising: The practice of architecture is a utilitarian art that seeks inspiration from many muses. It is not a fine art created in the relative solace of the studio, but a rather messy art, influenced by many voices and compromised by many forces before it is finally realized. In this light, it is no wonder that some confusion might reign.

There are, however, useful distinctions to be made between the three terms, and one might start with the first of the three: Mission Style. At its most basic, Mission Style obviously refers to architectural elements that were typical of the mission buildings that originally inspired it (Fig. 1). With more direct connections to the late-eighteenth and early-nineteenth-century Spanish Conquest, Father Junipero Serra's mission-building program for the king of Spain, which began in 1769, and the later churches of Mexico, the Southwest and Alta California, it seems that Mission Style became most prevalent during a period from roughly 1890 to 1920. It was characterized by thick plaster adobe walls, front doorways embellished with baroque or *churrigueresque*

FIG.2

ornamentation, and symmetrical curved gable end façades that projected above the roof, often stepping up from the sides to bell towers or arched bell niches and a central curved arch or pediment. Rather heavy in scale, the Mission Style appears to have been more popular for public rather than private buildings. There are a few residential examples, but many more Southern California churches, railroad stations, hotels and banks that adopted this style (Fig.2).

The second term, Spanish Colonial, on the other hand, is not so connected in its inspiration to the Spanish Conquest, Mexico, or our native Southwest traditions as one might suppose. Instead, during its heyday from approximately 1920 to 1930, it looked back more specifically to Spain itself, particularly areas of Southern Spain where the architecture had in turn developed Islamic characteristics influenced by Moorish occupations prior to the sixteenth century. The rural farmhouses of Andalusia (Fig.3) were often a favorite reference for many architects who chose to work in Southern California, preeminent among them George Washington Smith in Santa Barbara, Wallace Neff in Los Angeles, and Reginald Johnson in Pasadena. Their versions of Spanish Colonial architecture were frequently characterized by asymmetrical, undecorated façades (Fig.4). A picturesque simplicity was often at the heart of the appeal of these Andalusian examples. As Sexton noted in his 1926 book, *Spanish Influence on American Architecture*, "The peasant dwelling, or farmhouse of Spain, offers, perhaps, most for adaptation to American needs. Its chief characteristic lies in a pleasing combination of simplicity and dignity."

Spanish Colonial, however, which related more specifically to Spain, was only one of the stylistic impulses contained in the third term: Mediterranean Style. Mediterranean is a broader term and implies not just influences from Spain, but potentially from many other regions bordering the Mediterranean Sea, including Southern France, Italy, Sicily, Majorca, Morocco, Greece, and others. For most of us, examples based on Renaissance-era Italian villas are probably most recognizable (Fig.5), but the Southern French farmhouse (Fig.6) and the whitewashed architecture of the Greek Aegean Islands (Fig.7) are also related to the family. Perhaps it should properly be retitled Mediterranean *Styles*.

In Southern California, beginning about 1915, the blossoming of the Mediterranean Style in architecture was to alter the face of many communities, and in places like Santa Barbara, literally transform them. What came to be called the Mediterranean Revival became a

FIG.3

FIG.3 *Farm House Near Penarubia, Province of Malaga, Spain. Image originally published in Winsor Soule's* Spanish Farm Houses and Minor Public Buildings *(New York: Architectural Book Publishing Co., 1924), p. 10.*

FIG.4 *Heberton Residence, Santa Barbara, California, c. 1918. George Washington Smith, Architect. Photo by Frances Benjamin Johnston. Image originally published in the July 1923 issue of* The Architect, *Plate CXIX. Architecture and Design Collection of the University Art Museum, University of California, Santa Barbara.*

FIG.5 *The Villetta, at the Villa Palmieri, San Domenico, Italy. Thirteenth century. Photo by Harold Donaldson Eberlein. Image originally published in Harold Donaldson Eberlein's* Villas of Florence and Tuscany *(Philadelphia: J. B. Lippincott Co., 1922), p. 194.*

craze of significant proportions, celebrated in dozens of newspapers and magazine articles. To quote the late historian David Gebhard from his 1964 book on the work of George Washington Smith, "In the twentieth-century American architectural scene, there has been only one brief period of time and only one restricted geographic area in which there existed anything approaching a unanimity of architectural form. This was the period, from approximately 1920 through the early 1930s, when the Spanish Colonial or the Mediterranean Revival was virtually the accepted norm in Southern California." The changes in the architectural landscape that this occasioned were so popular and pervasive that they still affect us today. Whole communities would be designed around Mediterranean themes. Although many of them have since been diluted by other stylistic impulses, centers such as Santa Barbara, Palos Verdes, Ojai, and Rancho Santa Fe, as well as a host of newer community developments, continue to enforce architectural guidelines that are based on Mediterranean styles.

It is important to reiterate that the Mediterranean Revival, as distinct from the Mission Style or Spanish Colonial, drew from a broader range and scale of influences from different European sources, and it is very likely this variety that made it admirably suitable for residential applications. Like the Spanish Colonial, it was a revival not of indigenous or local architectural traditions, but one inspired by far off Spanish, Italian, Moroccan, and other examples. How did this distant European connection come to pass in the late "pioneer" days of Southern California? One would not necessarily have assumed, culturally at least, so direct a connection between California and Europe.

At the end of the nineteenth century, Southern California was becoming an

FIG.4

increasingly appealing tourist destination for those from the Midwestern and Eastern United States. Some towns, such as Santa Barbara, had become attractive resort communities and vacation havens for the elite, boasting major hotels and a number of rentable residential estates and villas. Many of these early visitors from New York, Philadelphia, Chicago, and other major metropolitan areas were affluent, educated travelers who had been to Europe. A few of them were also architects who had trained at the École des Beaux-Arts in Paris and had made what was called the "grand tour," an artistic pilgrimage to countries like Italy, France, and Spain to be introduced firsthand to the Classical art and architecture they had studied and, in the process, the vernacular architecture of the places they visited along the way.

When these sophisticated visitors came to Southern California, they recognized a familiar Mediterranean-like

FIG.5

environment. If they were from Chicago or New York and visited during the cold winter months, the sunshine likely made an even greater impression on them. Starting in the 1880s, many decided to build winter residences in places like Pasadena, Santa Barbara, and Palos Verdes. They and their architects frequently brought picturesque, romantic architectural visions to this new Eden that were clearly inspired by their travels to similar climates and settings in the Mediterranean. A number of them eventually decided to stay year round. They would make new lives by adopting a new lifestyle in a place that, while civilized and safe, still seemed foreign and exotic enough to invite the indulgence of their dreams. As Gebhard observed in his 1989 essay on the architect Wallace Neff, "With the majority of architects and clients of the '20s and '30s, there was an overall desire to immerse oneself in some romantically conceived episode of the distant past or to be magically transported to some exotic, faraway place."

For some, California also clearly offered attractive business opportunities. These wealthy newcomers, along with a few families that had established roots there earlier and prospered, were not rough western pioneers prospecting for gold. Instead, they saw investment opportunities in oil and real estate and other areas of growth. But the attraction of the place itself, the thing that led to their indulging their romantic fantasies in building Mediterranean dream houses, was that it was relatively undeveloped land with spectacular mountain and ocean settings that offered a chance to start over, unencumbered by the relatively staid cultural and architectural traditions of the East. In his 1875 *Transatlantic Sketches*, Henry James observed California as "a sort of prepared but unconscious Italy, the primitive *plate*, in perfect condition, but with the impressions of History all yet to be made."

FIG.6 *Farmhouse, Southern France. Photo by Marc Appleton.*

FIG.7 *Oia, Santorini, Greece. Photo by Marc Appleton.*

FIG.6

FIG.7

Many of these new, well-heeled settlers and their architects not only had been to Europe as tourists or students, but when they designed their new California homes they returned there, not just to revisit places of inspiration in Spain, Italy, and France, but to actually collect and purchase materials, fixtures, and other architectural elements for the construction of their future homes. The light fixtures and ceramic tiles one sees in the original California Mediterranean Style houses from the 1920s were often imported from Sevilla, Tunisia, or other European tile and fixture centers, not Mexico. These materials eventually inspired local manufacturers, like the Malibu Potteries started by the Adamson family (see Adamson Residence, p. 54), but Europe was initially the prime marketplace for those who could afford the journey.

For those who could not afford the luxury of seeing the original in person, there soon became available an easier and more accessible source of design inspiration: architectural photography books. Travel books illustrated by hand drawings and etchings were quite common by the nineteenth century, but in the twentieth the technology of photography had advanced to such an extent that many travelers to Europe, including a number of architects, were returning with photographs suitable enough for publication. Books on Spanish architecture and decoration by Arthur and Mildred Stapley Byne were among some of the first. The Bynes also became well-known antiquarians and assisted many homeowners, including the owners of Casa del Herrero (see page 36), in acquiring and shipping back architectural materials and period furniture. A number of books copiously illustrated with examples of Mediterranean and Spanish architecture, including both the original European buildings and their

American colonial offspring, soon became available: Winsor Soule's *Spanish Farm Houses and Minor Public Buildings* (1924), R. W. Sexton's *Spanish Influence on American Architecture* (1926), Rexford Newcomb's *The Spanish House for America* (1927), *Mediterranean Domestic Architecture in the United States* (1928), Richard Requa's *Architectural Details, Spain and the Mediterranean* (1927), *Old Work Inspiration for American Architecture* (1929), and Philip H. Staat's *California Architecture in Santa Barbara* (1929). The last of these, Staat's book, had actually been commissioned in the aftermath of Santa Barbara's devastating 1925 earthquake as a source book to promote continued architectural development of the city according to acceptable Spanish Revival guidelines. Widely read at the time, most of these books have long been out of print, although some have recently been reprinted. At the time, they served a purpose every bit as valuable as the architectural "style" and practical "how to" books of today for the new homebuilder.

Compatible with the importation of foreign architectural influences was the cultivation of a landscape of largely Mediterranean plant varieties. The cypress, stone pine, olive, citrus, eucalyptus, and palm trees we have since come to associate with Southern California are all foreign species originally imported from Europe, Australia, and other parts of the world. In this benign climate with its rich soil, water was all that was needed to spur the development of gardens that would be suitably exotic and harmonious with their houses. The palette of plant material in many of these gardens mirrors its Mediterranean equivalent: succulents, boxwood, laurel, lavender, rosemary, thyme, and many other varieties. Most of the houses were designed to reinforce the garden spaces around them, as gardens were a year-round affair. Seasonal changes in other parts of the country might have their own magic garden moments, but the moment in a place like Southern California can last all year long.

Mediterranean architectural influences brought with them more open gestures to the garden. Loggias, porches, courtyards, patios and terraces were common features providing opportunities not just for arrival, but also for sitting, socializing, and dining al fresco throughout the year. Pergolas, fountains, and other features were often used as axial focal points or destinations for paths or lawns that extended the interior circulation and principal rooms of the houses out into the landscape. The "outdoor room" Spanish garden of Casa del Herrero (Fig.8 and page 36) is but one example of this.

It is by all these connections between architecture and landscape, both direct and indirect, that California and the Mediterranean were related. This was not merely some notion that Southern California was "like" the Mediterranean in climate and setting, but that many houses and gardens drew direct inspiration, and indeed in many cases actual materials, from their Mediterranean counterparts, specific foreign places with which their owners and architects were already familiar or had visited. As the Mediterranean Revival in California further developed, however, it began feeding on itself. As already noted above, many of the books published in the 1920s were now of contemporary Spanish Colonial and Mediterranean houses in California and Florida, not Europe. Most of these houses were not slavish copies of the originals, but more locally interpretive and eclectic. At the time, even historians like Rexford Newcomb recognized, in the colonization of Mediterranean influences, the tendency to mix elements from different sources. As stated in his book *Mediterranean Domestic Architecture in the United States*, he considered this an inevitable and natural result of their absorption into the American setting: "Spanish, Italian, Moorish, Byzantine—Mediterranean types generally—instead of being kept archeologically segregated, are under this orchestral process merged, as were those of golden threads of long ago, into a new sun-loving style which, while eminently American in its plan and utilities, is nevertheless distinctly

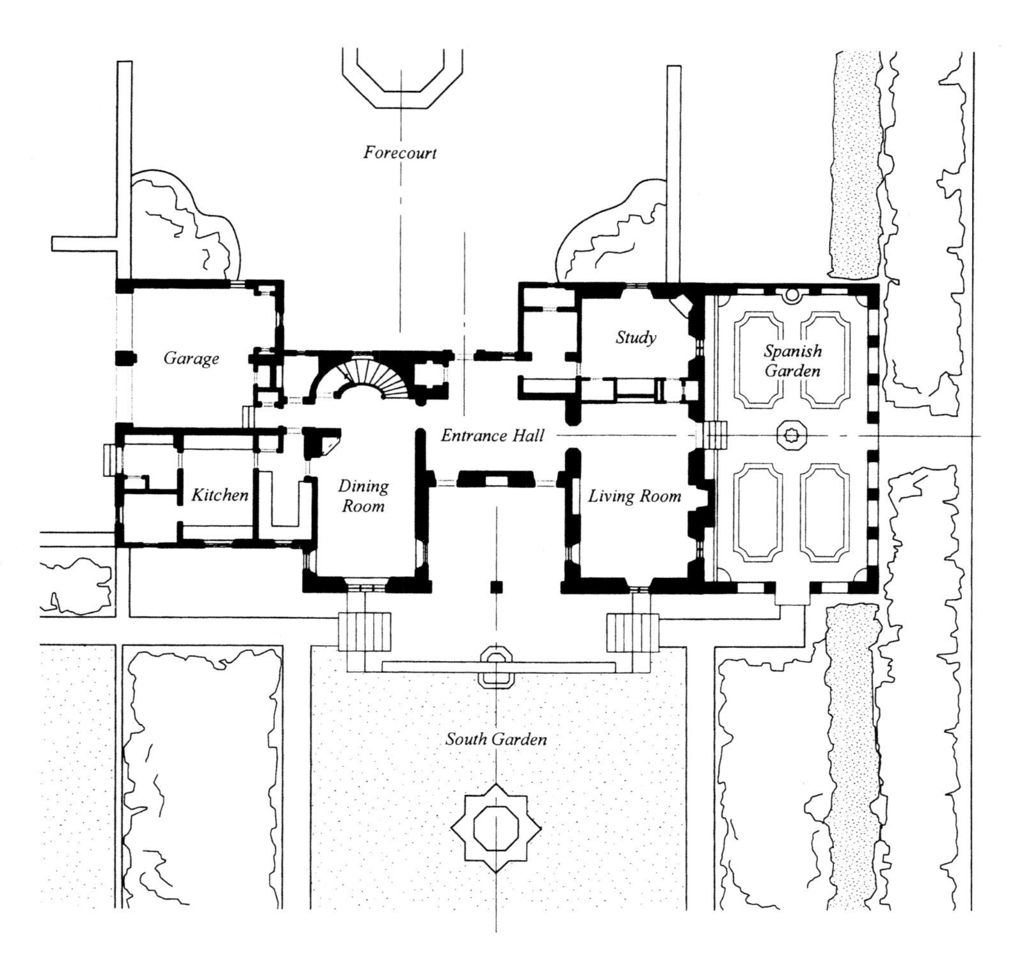

FIG.8 *Plan of Casa del Herrero, 1925. Geroge Washington Smith, Architect. Drawing by Appleton & Associates, Inc., Architects.*

Mediterranean in its origins and spirit." The Mediterranean Revival became an eclectic movement not only because of the variety of stylistic influences but because colonization gave it license to experiment and adapt to its new surroundings.

In the decades following the Mediterranean Revival in Southern California, we have not witnessed a period of architectural development as rich or intense as its heyday during the 1920s. The Depression, industrialization, and modern culture as we know it were soon to overtake us. The decline of individual craftsmanship in construction that was so central to both the successful design and execution of earlier Mediterranean Revival homes was imminent. The making of those houses had involved a cooperative process where everyone paid great attention to the materials and details. The sophistication of the clients and the shared knowledge and skill in the construction industry that had led to a more harmonious working relationship among client, architect, draftsman, contractor, and artisan were to change with the advent of machine-made, mass-produced, and cheaper, but more limited, products and materials.

Despite this decline, our fascination with Mediterranean architecture has survived, and its magic endures. It is still the most predominant stylistic impulse at work in Southern California's current housing market. The tragedy today is that it is executed so poorly, both in terms of design and construction. Architects, landscape designers, and builders have lost the shared knowledge and understanding of the historic Mediterranean architecture from which they were once inspired to create such stunningly beautiful offspring, and they no longer have as many sympathetic clients committed to supporting the level of quality that would be required.

Because of its continued influence, this book attempts not only to remember that golden age of Mediterranean Revival architecture, but also to celebrate a rich variety of houses in different styles, built in different parts of Southern California at different times. Some are large estates, some significantly smaller and more modest. Some are now historic museums or foundations open to the public, others are private residences built and/or occupied by owners who continue to make them a vital part of their daily lives. Each of the houses has a unique relationship to the landscape that, as is typical of most California Mediterranean houses, recognizes the importance of the garden as an active extension of the life inside. For many homeowners in Southern California, their gardens are sanctuaries every bit as sacred as their houses, and in some cases more so. Despite, or perhaps even because of, the hectic pace of modern civilization, these places still beckon to us, just as they did in an earlier time.

YUST RESIDENCE

Los Angeles, 1921

500

PREVIOUS PAGES *The front façade features false painted window frames typical of Tuscan houses.*

ABOVE *The richly detailed front door was carved on site by Italian artisans.*

RIGHT *Each room in the house was designed with a different ceiling. Here, groin vaults add drama to the dining room. The prints are from the Caldas/Humboldt Expedition to Colombia in the early nineteenth century.*

The very day Larry and Clara Yust bought their house, Clara looked out an upstairs window and, upon seeing the overgrown walled garden of the house next door, she exclaimed, "I want that house." They waited 20 years, in the process befriending their neighbor and the owner of the property at that time, Owen Churchill, before finally purchasing it from Mr. Churchill's estate in 1986.

The house, they both point out, simply needed restoration more than renovation or remodeling. Originally designed in 1921 by F. Pierpont Davis for his own family, the original Italian Renaissance style and floor plan of the villa needed little change to suit the Yusts, but it did require significant forensics and repainting to bring it back closer to its original condition.

PREVIOUS PAGES *Library shelves entirely cover two walls and were built by the owners to match the preexisting architecture of the living room. The original ceiling panels were painted by Italian artists.*

LEFT *The loggia has a built-in sofa and offers a cool retreat on hot afternoons.*

ABOVE *A decorated niche in the loggia. The walls are painted with dry pigment, typical of Tuscan houses.*

To accommodate their library, Larry added full-height stained wood shelves to the living room that complement the original hand-painted coffered wood ceiling. Their daughter Victoria, an architect, assisted with remodeling the kitchen and other improvements, but the exterior details and basic layout of the original adobe structure remained intact.

It was the formal garden that needed to be more seriously overhauled. Here, too, the original structure of the garden, including the major pathways, central fountain and boxwood hedges, had survived, but the rest, as Clara says, "was an overgrown mess." In reviving the garden, she worked with the original bones to create four distinct but interconnected garden areas: the main formal parterre garden, the secret garden, the orchard,

TOP *A fountain in the formal garden is inscribed with the year the house was completed—1921.*

ABOVE *A wooden porch off the master bedroom overlooks the formal garden.*

TOP RIGHT *One of two statues in the formal garden; the background color in the niche is original to the house.*

OPPOSITE *A view from the loggia into the secret garden reveals a fountain made from the capital of a Corinthian column left over from a church the architect was building at the time.*

and the *bosco* or forest, this last area experienced by a pathway around the outer edge of the formal garden through a dense canopy of eucalyptus, fir, and California Oak trees.

F. Pierpont Davis and his brother, Walter S. Davis, were the architects for some of Los Angeles's most charming and romantic courtyard apartments, and fully understood the value of the garden courtyard as an oasis, an outdoor "living room" and an extension of the life of the house. As viewed from the loggia below or balcony above, the Yusts' courtyard gardens offer seductive vistas, inviting one out to stroll the garden paths, wander the byways and corners, or pause and sit to take in its colors, smells and sounds. In a sense, the gardens are a series of different architectural spaces, each inviting you to explore the next, and it is perhaps this experience that Clara Yust's resurrection has so successfully achieved. The Davis family would feel as much at home today as they did in 1921, indeed even more so since ripeness and maturity are qualities a garden achieves only with the passage of time.

MONTALBA

Santa Barbara, 1995

PREVIOUS PAGES *A view of the islands over aloes in the gravel yard on the east side of the house.*

ABOVE *View of main entrance gallery.*

RIGHT *The dining room with its eighteenth-century ceiling beams. A collection of seventeenth- and eighteenth-century Spanish monks chairs line the walls facing a rustic table.*

Inveterate collectors George Schoellkopf and Gerald Incandela already had a 250-year-old house in Connecticut, and were looking to find a second winter home in Santa Barbara when, in 1994, they stumbled upon an empty, windswept hilltop property with panoramic views of the Pacific Ocean and surrounding mountains. A previous owner had gone as far as pouring a foundation for a house, but the couple bulldozed it, preferring to start fresh with their own plans.

Gerald, an internationally recognized photographer, and George, who was an antiques dealer with a Madison Avenue gallery in New York, joke that this new house actually pretends to be even older than their Connecticut house: "Perhaps a very déclassé move by today's trends," George remarks. Not only is it filled with architectural elements and relics salvaged from different places and times,

ABOVE *A twelfth-century French marble portal frames a hallway.*

RIGHT *The main sitting room includes an assemblage of antiques. The limestone floor and fireplace are from Burgundy and the library table in the foreground from Italy.*

but even the new materials have been carefully chosen to exude a patina of age. As a result, the house indeed has an ancient quality that belies its youth.

In the beginning, this was a challenge for some of the workmen, who were incredulous when Gerald suggested using their weathered, cement-covered scaffolding boards for a bedroom ceiling. As the construction progressed, however, the contractors were won over by their clients' insistent vision and got into the swing of things. When he was interviewed by them, architect Don Nulty graciously deferred to their blunt initial question as to whether or not he had a big ego, understanding that his clients had very strong ideas about what they wanted. It was, George says, an unexpectedly cooperative effort throughout the process given the fact that everything was custom made at their direction.

The house, designed around two adjacent inner courtyards, has a slightly monastic feel, which adds to the aura of age. Its rooms are organized around

LEFT *The bell tower overlooks the myrtle hedges and bay laurel, standards of the Cloister garden.*

BELOW LEFT *An old stonecutter's table sits in front of an antique Mexican door surround. The playful brick cornice above leads to the striped kitchen wall of California adobe and Mexican brick.*

RIGHT *Hundreds of Mexican roof tiles encircle a view of the Cloister garden, as seen from the bell tower.*

FOLLOWING PAGES *The view to the southeast, toward the garden house, overlooks the terrace of lemon trees in Tuscan terra cotta pots and the box parterre garden.*

these courtyards and look out over the gardens and countryside towards spectacular ocean views. An open loggia off the entry court offers a fireplace with outdoor seating protected against the wind, which at times on the property can rival a French mistral. One of the gardeners, who had a rail-thin physique, reported at one point that when a fierce wind came up he had to literally crawl back to his car to escape being blown off the hilltop.

It is perhaps fitting then, on a site so bleak and exposed, that Montalba has taken on the air of something that has weathered the years. Its design also suggests an organic growth over time, a stone wing here, a terracotta brick or plaster section there. In point of fact, it continues to be a work in progress. Horse stables and a cactus garden have just recently been added, and it seems as if the house's owners have successfully attempted, in their words, "to give a soul and feeling to each part," that excites one's imagination. Even the various gardens are developed like a sequence of outdoor rooms, each with its own identity expressed by George's layout and horticultural choices.

Although they modestly contend that the "house just did itself," there is a magic to the place that owes a significant debt to their elegant taste and intuitively felicitous partnership and collaboration. The combination of so many eclectic pieces in less capable hands could have been a messy disaster. Here it all seems to fit together harmoniously and unselfconsciously to create a charming and uniquely romantic place that, despite its newness, transcends the present.

CASA DEL HERRERO

Montecito, 1925

PREVIOUS PAGES *A tropical forest of strelitzia (giant bird-of-paradise) screens the entry court.*

RIGHT *In the dining room, a corner fireplace copied from the fourteenth-century Guadamor Castle in Toledo, Spain, bears Steedman's logo. A Gothic four-panel painting depicting the martyrdom of San Lorenzo hangs on the wall beyond a table set with antique Spanish Talavera china.*

Casa del Herrero (House of the Blacksmith) is one of the few Spanish Colonial homes left that today retains most of its original architecture, interiors and landscaping, thanks in large part to the generosity of the original family's heirs. The estate, including all of its furnishings, was transferred in 1994 to The Casa del Herrero Foundation to maintain it in perpetuity.

The original owners, George F. and Carrie Steedman, shared a passion for Santa Barbara and things Spanish. Mr. Steedman was a successful industrialist from St. Louis, but also a designer, silversmith, metalworker, engineer, inventor, amateur photographer, and man of many talents. Following World War I, he and his wife decided to build a retreat in Santa Barbara and in 1922 purchased an 11-acre parcel off East Valley Road in Montecito with ocean and mountain views. That same year, they hired local architect George Washington Smith to design their house.

Mr. Steedman was, to say the least, a very interested and involved client, and maintained an insightful critical dialogue as the design evolved. A lengthy correspondence between client and architect attests to his demanding program, and refinements and additions to the house were still being discussed when Smith died in 1930. Lutah Maria Riggs, Smith's assistant, skillfully added a tiny octagonal library tower in 1931.

The Steedmans' commitment to creating an authentic Spanish home included trips starting in 1923 to Spain and Tunisia, where they were assisted by the

BELOW *A second floor sleeping porch features an aubergine tile border, hand-painted door surrounds with ziggurat designs, and an old Spanish tile floor.*

RIGHT *The aluminum and copper furniture in the loggia was designed by Steedman.*

antiquarians and authors Arthur and Mildred Stapley Byne in purchasing numerous items, including ceramic tiles, doors, ceilings, and antique furniture. Many of these elements found their way into the design and construction of the house, and as a result the house has an ancestral feeling enhanced by the presence of the Medieval and Renaissance-era furniture and furnishings.

The architecture of the house was clearly influenced not only by Andalusian Spanish-Moorish precedents but also by Italian villa architecture, particularly on the south-facing garden front. Here, Smith played with scale by varying the sizes of the arched openings and windows in a way that imparts a miniaturized grandeur to the façade. The same playfulness is at work on the interior, where many of the rooms, while actually quite small, give the impression of a significantly grander scale due to the abundance of sumptuous decoration and rich furnishings.

The gardens were a particular focus of the owner's attention over many years. Originally laid out from a plan by Ralph Stevens, they were further developed with input from Lockwood de Forest, as well as the horticulturalist Peter Reidel. Although the main house was substantially completed by 1925 (on June 29th, in fact, the day of the great Santa Barbara earthquake), the gardens did not reach their fruition until 1933.

ABOVE *A polychrome tile fountain in the fern garden provides a focal point on the main garden axis.*

FACING PAGE *A view through the vine-covered arcade of the Spanish garden patio reveals an exedra with its tiled Tree of Life panel framed by polychrome tile benches.*

FOLLOWING PAGES *The rear façade of the house and its loggia face the south garden lawn and its Moorish-inspired eight-pointed star fountain. The walled Spanish garden is behind the arcade to the right.*

There is a strong cross-axial organization to the house that connects inside to outside, and one of the delightful aspects of this is that the exterior elevations of the house, and the courtyard and garden spaces they face, have a distinctly unique character on each of the four sides. At the front of the house, an entry courtyard and fountain modeled after those at the Alhambra in Granada, Spain, are formal gestures, but the front elevation of the house is quite asymmetrical and informal in its composition.

On the opposite garden front, the loggia is centered on the main garden axis and its water feature of interconnected tiled rivulets and basins, but it is two instead of three bays wide, with a column rather than an opening at the center. The side windows here also are diminutive in scale and asymmetrically placed, subtly tweaking an otherwise symmetrical composition in plan.

To the east, the living room opens onto a walled outdoor garden with arched openings defining the space and providing vistas through to the adjacent lawn and tiled excedra. This garden "room" would only need a roof to be literally another part of the house and is a successful example of an outdoor space that has an enclosed, "indoor" atmosphere. On the opposite side, a cobbled service courtyard off the kitchen adjacent to Steedman's magnificent metal workshop exhibits the much more informal, casual character of an Andalusian farmhouse, where a playful juxtaposition of gutters, downspouts, steps, a tiled washbasin, and other elements are more playfully composed. In this way, Casa del Herrero is a hallmark for the interplay between symmetry in plan and asymmetry in elevation, becoming an exemplar of one of the eclectic nuances of the Spanish Colonial Revival.

Open to the public by reservation on Wednesdays and Saturdays from February to mid-December, Casa del Herrero offers a uniquely detailed glimpse back in time and also the experience of appreciating how skillfully house and garden can be interrelated.

SERRANIA

Montecito, 1924

Restoration and interiors by John Saladino.

PREVIOUS PAGES *A view of the entrance elevation from the auto court.*

RIGHT *The great room features the original redwood panels and ceiling, which were carefully restored after having been painted over.*

Restoration and interiors by John Saladino.

Louis F. and Ida May Swift, who had fallen in love with the Santa Barbara area on a winter visit from Chicago, continued for almost 20 years to rent houses during their regular winter visits while dabbling in real estate purchases that never seemed appealing enough to settle on. Finally, in 1917, Swift purchased 40 acres in the foothills of Montecito, followed later that same year by an additional 700-acre purchase of adjacent mountain range, eventually growing to a total of approximately 1,500 acres. In 1922, however, Ida May Swift died, and Swift spent increasingly less time in Santa Barbara.

Designed by the local architectural firm of Soule, Hastings & Murphy and built in the mid–1920s after Ida's death, Swift originally planned Serrania (Mountainous Region) as a hunting lodge and future guest house to a larger main house that was itself never built. It had four bedrooms and maids' quarters upstairs, with three guest suites downstairs. The second floor had a long cantilevered wooden porch similar to Monterey Colonial houses, which wrapped three sides of the bedroom wing and provided views out over the hillside to the Santa Barbara harbor and ocean beyond. Also on the second floor at the front of the house was a large, redwood-paneled hall of baronial proportions with a central fireplace and wood trusses supporting a high, beamed ceiling.

Restoration and interiors by John Saladino.

Restoration and interiors by John Saladino.

Swift died in Chicago in 1937. With the Depression, the value of his estate had dwindled and his Montecito holdings were sold in probate. In the decades that followed, the property, like most large parcels throughout the area, was subdivided, and the house changed ownership several times, accumulating several outbuildings and undergoing successive remodelings. When Tim and Audrey Fisher acquired it in 2000, they hired designer John Saladino to assist in a comprehensive restoration.

Saladino considers the essence of his contribution to be "removing the desecrations of the last 50 years." The redwood of the grand hall, he laments, had been painted over white, and a sunken bar had been installed at one end. "The first floor entrance to the house was a mess," he says. "There was no place to go in and, once in, no obvious direction to go."

Restoration and interiors by John Saladino.

To remedy matters, the Fishers and Saladino gutted the first floor entry area, creating a new façade and entrance hall with a stairway up to the great room on the second floor. The great room was laboriously stripped of paint back to the original redwood; the sunken bar removed; and French doors installed out to a small new ocean view terrace—"the prow of the ship," as Saladino calls it. At the first floor, this terrace structure also created a new ceremonial front porch for the house and gateway to the garden.

With the assistance of landscape architect Sydney Baumgartner, the 1950s-era swimming pool was replaced by a new pool on a lower terrace, allowing the upper terrace adjacent to the house to be restored to an expansive lawn that connects around the end of the house up to a new garden area off the dining room terrace. Here, Saladino installed an operable wall of bronze-framed glass doors that turned the new dining room into an area that feels more outside than in.

Uphill from the house, an old stone water reservoir that dates back to the original construction was turned into a media room below with an exercise room and office for Mr. Fisher above. Further up the hill an old wood frame structure was remodeled as a new guest cottage. To tie all this together and create a more ceremonial approach to the house from the street below, the abandoned original driveway was reopened and planted with additional olive trees. There is now the feeling to one's arrival that this place has somehow always been this way. Saladino says it was simply the challenge of "making order out of chaos," but the order is a natural one that has enhanced rather than altered one's sense of history.

FACING PAGE TOP *The new dining room is enclosed by bronze framed doors, which open to the upper terrace and garden area.*

FACING PAGE BOTTOM *The great room.*

ABOVE *In the lower entrance hall, old limestone floors, stone walls, and beams are in contrast to the great room above.*

FOLLOWING PAGES
TOP LEFT *A pergola separating the pool and tennis court leads up to the main house lawn.*

BOTTOM LEFT *A trellis covers the dining room patio to create an outdoor room.*

RIGHT *Stone, black pebbles, and yellow brick define a small breakfast patio.*

Restoration and interiors by John Saladino.

Restoration and interiors by John Saladino.

Restoration and interiors by John Saladino.

ADAMSON RESIDENCE

Malibu, 1930

PREVIOUS PAGES *The ocean front of the house looks eastward over the Sunrise Patio to a lawn and gardens, and the Malibu Pier.*

LEFT *Wrought-iron loggia doors under a second floor balcony lead out to the Sunrise Patio. The balconies are an extension of the loggia ceiling inside.*

When one visits the Adamson House on busy Pacific Coast Highway in the center of popular Malibu, it is hard to imagine the 13,000-acre "farm near the ocean under the lee of the mountain, with a trout brook, wild trees, a lake, good soil and excellent climate," that Frederick H. Rindge described when he purchased it in 1892 from Henry Keller. Today, the area is a congested beach community with local residents, surfers, and tourists crowding the scene, but at the time Rindge purchased Rancho Malibu, there were no roads to it, only access by horseback or boat, and it must have been the spectacular seaside setting that led him to call it the "American Riviera."

The peaceful "farm" would not be long for this world. Soon after Rindge's purchase, the Southern Pacific Railroad tried to intrude on his paradise with plans to build a railroad along the coast connecting Los Angeles to Santa Barbara. Rindge acted quickly by incorporating his own company, the Hueneme, Malibu, and Port Los Angeles Railroad, and successfully blocked Southern Pacific's attempt. This would not, however, be the end of pressures from the outside world. When Rindge died in 1905, his widow Rhoda May Knight Rindge was forced to continue the fight, this time against the county and state's desire to construct a major highway through Malibu.

May Rindge, as she was known, was an enterprising woman, and appointed Merritt Huntley Adamson, a well-educated farmer with a law degree from USC, as superintendent of Malibu Ranch. Merritt soon became a member of the family when he married May's daughter, Rhoda, in 1915, and they subsequently established a successful dairy, Adohr Farms (Adohr is Rhoda spelled backwards), which at one time was considered the largest in the state. In her continuing struggles against the state's highway plans and to offset mounting legal expenses, May began the development of the now famous Malibu Colony. She also discovered large deposits of red clay on the property and hired Rufus B. Keeler to establish a pottery in 1926, a venture that became the legendary Malibu

ABOVE *The teakwood and bottle glass front door is framed with an urn-of-flowers design.*

FACING PAGE *The Moorish arch living room and dining room windows are faced with tile in an elaborate floral design.*

ABOVE *A Persian rug design in tile on the loggia floor is composed of 674 custom tiles created by William Handley during the short 6 years that Malibu Potteries existed.*

RIGHT *The living room features a basket weave floor tile design and a fireplace opening that echoes the arched Moorish window.*

Potteries, which produced the colorful tiles that became a popular architectural feature in many Southern California buildings and gardens.

Alas, these successes could not prevent the march of progress across their lands, and in 1926, the same year the pottery was established, the state finally prevailed in obtaining a right-of-way. The Roosevelt Highway, now known as Pacific Coast Highway, was opened to the public in 1926. Ironically, the future intensity of this intrusion was not enough at the time to deter the family from constructing a house on Vacquero Hill near Malibu Creek's ocean outlet at Malibu Lagoon, and also adjacent to the new highway.

In 1927, they hired Stiles O. Clements from the well-known architectural firm of Morgan, Walls & Clements to design a Spanish-Moorish house, which was originally to be a part-time beach house

but which in 1936 became the Adamson's permanent home. Completed in 1930, the house is perhaps understandably a shrine of sorts to Malibu tile, which was used excessively throughout.

From one's arrival at the front of the house, where tile lines the arched openings of the front door and windows above, on into the interiors, upstairs, downstairs and outside again to the patios and fountains that grace the gardens, the presence of tile is everywhere. Even the Persian "rug" on the loggia floor, replete with fringe, is made of Malibu tile. The bathrooms, as might be expected, are showcases that include complete floors, walls, and ceilings in tile. The kitchen, where the designs were purportedly inspired by Native American motifs, is a stunning Art Deco exercise in blues, reds, yellows, and blacks. Tile is used to trim arches and openings, form tabletops, create bases, and even to celebrate a kitchen wall clock. In an otherwise informal landscape designed by Dewitt Norris, the spectacular tiled Peacock Fountain at the rear patio and the Star Fountain beyond dominate a view of the beach. Even the flowerpots have been glazed so that there is no mistaking to whose house they belong.

To complement this exuberant display of ceramics, interior designer John Holzclaw added reproductions of Spanish furniture, while Danish artists Ejnar Hansen and Peter Nielsen decorated ceilings, fireplace mantles, and other elements with stencil and hand-painted designs that add a slightly Scandinavian flair to the proceedings.

In 1968, the property was purchased by the California Department of Parks and Recreation, which had plans to demolish the house to create a public park. In an ironic parallel to the Rindge and Adamson families' earlier battles against the county and state, the Malibu Historical Society fought for 14 years to save the house and property, finally succeeding in obtaining National Historic Landmark status. Today it is open to the public for tours as the Malibu Lagoon Museum.

FACING PAGE *A colorfully titled dining nook off the kitchen was used by the cook and chauffeur. Ma Tilija poppies painted on the ceiling are the work of Danish artists Ejmar Hausen and Peter Nielsen, part of the team of artists that completed the original interior of the house.*

ABOVE *Off the living room in the Sunset Patio, an urn-of-flowers motif crowns the tiled panel above French doors and below a wrought-iron potted plant shelf.*

TOP *A wall spigot in a bathroom suggests a fountain rather than a sink.*

ABOVE *One of four remaining large pots shows the* cuerda seca *or "dry line" glaze technique, and expresses the extraordinary talents of the original potters.*

RIGHT *The colorful tiled fountain off the Sunrise Patio is decorated with a Peacock motif. World famous Surfrider Beach is in the distance beyond.*

BROWN CONDOMINIUMS

Santa Barbara, 1933

Located in the charming historic neighborhood of the Paseo Viejo district in downtown Santa Barbara, this building has had quite a history. Louise Murphy Vhay, who owned much of the block, originally constructed the front portion in 1932 as a warehouse. In 1933, the freelance writer Robert "Bobby" McKee Hyde added a separate building at the back. Hyde and Channing Peake, an artist friend, allegedly used the property for an antique warehouse and art studio. In 1952, another owner connected the two buildings, and in the 1960s, when the neighborhood became a lively bohemian center of artistic activity and the happening place to be, wild parties were a weekly event in the courtyard.

When designer Micholyn Brown and her husband Fred Brown purchased the property in 1996, what had become a compound of four separate rental units was being occupied as a single residence. In the first phase of their project, the Browns interconnected the studios and installed new bathrooms and a kitchen. While living in the space, the Browns began contemplating the second phase of the project: the remodeling and additions that would accommodate a second dwelling unit at the rear. They enlisted architect Kirk B. Gradin, who helped realize plans for this phase of the project

PREVIOUS PAGES *100-year-old olive trees grace the central courtyard.*

ABOVE *A herringbone-pattern brick floor extends along one side of the central courtyard and is furnished as if it were an interior hallway.*

FACING PAGE *A stone* paseo *enclosed by wood stake walls and trellis beams leads from the street to a rear side entrance.*

FOLLOWING PAGES *Remodeling included this new living area and fireplace.*

CUBA

FACING PAGE *A kiva fireplace and French doors to a private patio improved an informal dining area.*

ABOVE *In the guest room, an antique stained glass window creates privacy from the street and sidewalk.*

that sensitively addressed both the historic character of the existing buildings and the complicated sloping site at the rear half of the property on which the new addition would be located.

The end result of the Browns and Gradin's efforts respected the historic front part of the complex with a two-story addition that stepped down at the back, placing the second story and garages on a lower level. In fact, when one enters the courtyard from the street, the new part appears to be an extension of the original single story and is almost unnoticed, retaining the lower scale and character of the original. A trellised walkway was added down the side to create a separate street entry, and a portion of the rear of the original building was cleverly absorbed into the new second unit.

The brick courtyard with its fountain offers a pleasantly inviting outdoor space shaded by two venerable olive trees that look even older than the original building. The building's porch was extended in an L-shape to embrace the court, and although new wood was needed for much of the remodeling, Fred Brown apparently spent hours treating and finishing it so it blended seamlessly with the old. Even though the structure is not true masonry construction, one nevertheless has the distinct feeling that it has been there for decades as one of Santa Barbara's historic adobe haciendas. What is particularly successful is that the Browns have achieved this on so small a lot in a very urban context, proving an expansive garden setting isn't always essential to creating a successful oasis.

VILLA NARCISSA

Rancho Palos Verdes, 1924

PREVIOUS PAGES *A view through the iron gates of the front entry courtyard garden.*

LEFT *Della Robbia glazed ceramic wall plaque imported from Tuscany creates a decorative arch over the front door.*

FACING PAGE *Inside the front entry hall, frescos of a Mediterranean garden recall the real garden just outside.*

FOLLOWING PAGES *Sixteenth-century walnut furniture complements the painted coffered ceiling in the living room.*

The Palos Verdes Peninsula just south of Los Angeles is a hillside setting overlooking the Pacific Ocean that reminds one of the coasts along southern France, Monaco or northern Italy. With a little imagination you could easily feel you were gazing down from the cliffs above the Mediterranean Sea. When successful New York banker Frank A. Vanderlip purchased 16,200 acres here in 1912 to develop what was to become Palos Verdes Estates and Rancho Palos Verdes, and hired Frederick Law Olmstead, Jr., to assist in the master plan, it is quite understandable that he turned to Italy for inspiration in designing his own Villa. High on a slope above the ocean at Portuguese Bend and reached by a long uphill driveway lined with pepper trees, Villa Narcissa, named after Vanderlip's wife, was built in the 1920s as the guest house for a much larger villa he had planned, which was patterned after the sixteenth-century Villa Giulia in Rome.

Hopes of building the main house died with the advent of the Depression, but the 12 acres with Villa Narcissa remained in the family, eventually passing in 1946 to Vanderlip's son, Kelvin Cox Vanderlip, as a wedding present for him and his new Norwegian bride, Elin. The couple had four children and expanded the original gardens, adding a number of outbuildings. Kelvin died in 1956, but Elin has continued living in the house, guarding a remarkable family legacy with stubborn resolve against the forces of twentieth-century suburban real estate development that are a far cry from the romantic, rural paradise her father-in-law and Olmstead had envisioned.

It is thanks to Elin's eccentric and obstinate dedication that Villa Narcissa has not lost its original magic. Although a bit neglected due to the increased costs of maintaining it, the garden is still an impressive sight, with its allée of mature Italian cypresses flanking the grand central stairs leading from the front door uphill to a Doric temple at the top. Overgrown terraces traverse back and forth on either side. The Hortensia terrace, inspired by one at the Villa Aldobrandini in Frascati, Italy, extends along the southern side of the house and still overlooks the descending hillside all the way to Catalina Island, where Elin and Kelvin first met. Terra-cotta pots, garden ornaments, and statues imported from Impruneta in Tuscany grace the parterre gardens, and peacocks and hens still roam the grounds. Although things are a bit rough around the edges, and untended

TOP *The Doll House, framed by terra-cotta statues imported from Impruneta, Italy, is an architectural miniature of the main house.*

ABOVE *Olive trees shade the brick covered Hortensia terrace that overlooks the ocean.*

RIGHT *On axis with the front door and entry courtyard garden, a grand stairway and Italian cypress allée ascends uphill to a Doric temple at the top.*

areas of the garden have gone to seed, the spirit of Italy and the Mediterranean is still alive and well here.

If they were proposed today, the bright red ochre walls and yellow window and door trim of the Villa would be bold enough to be emphatically turned down by any local design review board, but they somehow fit the setting, harmoniously conversing with the brick patios and walkways, terra-cotta ornaments, and the vividly colored plantings of bougainvillea and geraniums. This is an exuberant place befitting its mistress, and a unique and important historic landmark of California's Mediterranean Colonial tradition. Let us hope that it will survive to honor the Vanderlip family's remarkable achievement and inspire future visitors.

THE FARMSTEAD

Rancho Palos Verdes, 1931

PREVIOUS PAGES *The back of the house, with hayloft above on the left and bedroom loggia right, shows off the informal symmetry of Kafman's design.*

ABOVE *A large studio window in the living room looks out to a side terrace and garden.*

RIGHT *The living room is decorated with an eclectic mix of family heirlooms and antiques.*

E. Douglas Levinson, a lawyer for Frank A. Vanderlip's bank in New York and a partner in developing Portuguese Bend, purchased 40 acres for an elegant vacation retreat near Vanderlip's property (see Villa Narcissa, p. 72) on which he planned to build a grand villa and horse stables. In a scenario identical to Vanderlip's, Levinson only managed to build his stables, not the main residence that he had envisioned overlooking the ocean, which was to be connected inland via a long tree-lined allée to the stables.

The Tuscan-styled farm buildings, which included the horse stables, were designed in 1928 by the architect Gordon B. Kaufman, but not built until 1931. In addition to the stables, they included quarters for the farm manager and servants, garages and a hay loft, all arranged in a U-shaped compound around a gated central courtyard. Surrounding the compound were a lath house, kitchen gardens, and fruit orchards, which had been designed by noted landscape architect A.E. Hanson.

More than likely, Levinson was another victim of the Depression—he never completed his estate, nor lived in the farm buildings. In the 1950s, the 40-acre parcel was divided and sold, and eventually Skip and Ginia Warner purchased the farm buildings along with 4 acres. The Warners were sympathetic rural folks, and Ginia was apparently quite a character, an animal lover who believed The Farmstead to be a "peaceable kingdom" where she fed wild and domesticated animals alike and even built a little "hospital" in the woods especially for sick peacocks. Ginia Warner's ashes, along with those of many of their relatives and, one suspects, quite a few pets, are buried on the place, giving rise to suspicions that the farm is now haunted by friendly ghosts.

Arriving at The Farmstead today is indeed taking a step back in time, as it doubtless was in 1931 as well. The romantic setting designed by Kaufman and Hanson is still so compelling that

ABOVE *The side patio, off the living room, is a perfect spot for weekend brunches.*

RIGHT *An archway, flanked by a pair of potted kumquat trees, leads from the central court to the perennial garden beyond.*

one cannot help but feel transported to some early-nineteenth-century farm deep in the Tuscan countryside. The place acquired its third owners, Charles and Jean Shriver, in 1983, and they continue to live in this modest but idyllic setting with their son, daughter-in-law, and four grandchildren, much as their Italian family counterparts might have.

At the time the Shrivers took possession, however, the gardens were an overgrown, tangled wilderness and one of their first steps was to enlist landscape designer Julie Heinsheimer to help clean it up. In the process, they rediscovered the original shape of the garden. Hidden under the overgrown thickets were the original pathways and some of the original plantings, and confirming this was an A. E. Hanson plan they had found in the attic showing the orchards and garden parterres. Heinsheimer added four rose trellises and a grape arbor, which took its cues from the old lath house. Recently Ric Dykzeul has designed a layout for a new orchard to replace the tired old fruit trees. The garden has finally returned to some semblance of its former glory, with a few up-to-date improvements.

The interior of the buildings also underwent some restoration and remodeling. Intent on putting in a workable kitchen, the Shrivers hired architect and architectural historian Stefanos Polyzoides to design what proved to be a modest solution that was in harmony with Kaufman's humble aesthetic. The plaster colors the Shrivers have used to patch and repair are indistinguishable from the weathered patina of the original walls. Appropriately for a farm, everything is still a bit rough around the edges and perfectly imperfect.

The restraint the Shrivers have observed in attending to The Farmstead reflects their understanding and appreciation of the original romantic vision so skillfully realized by Levinson and his design team. One has the feeling that, in sensitive hands like the Shrivers, with just the right amount (but not too much) care, this time-worn vision will live forever in this place.

TOP *A lath house in one corner of the perennial garden.*

ABOVE *A whimsical peacock gate on the back patio. Real peacocks and hens roamed the estate in earlier times.*

RIGHT *A boxwood maze encircles a fountain and a small explosion of bird-of-paradise.*

LES OLIVIERS

Montecito, 1940s/1989

PREVIOUS PAGES *At the front of the house, old iron gates are used for the front door, and French blue shutters frame the windows.*

ABOVE *In the living room, shutters cover a window to the front courtyard. Old olive jars adorn an antique eighteenth-century commode.*

RIGHT *A large-scale herringbone terra-cotta floor and the warm tones of glazed walls and furniture create a soft, light-filled atmosphere.*

Once the only structure on the property, a 1940s Montecito cottage was located where the master bedroom suite currently sits. At one point, a kidney-shaped pool was added, and in the late 1980s a major addition and remodel occurred. By the time interior designer Lucinda Lester and her husband, Walter Owen, acquired the property in 1993, it had evolved into a somewhat characterless contractor's spec house.

Without significantly changing the footprint, the couple set about remodeling the building into a French country manor house they call Les Oliviers (The Olive Trees). They took off the front porch and in its place composed a more symmetrical front façade. To this affect, they added shutters to the windows and French doors, as well as new, classically framed glass and wrought-iron front doors made from a pair of old French gates. Where there should have been windows or shutters, trompe l'oeil versions were substituted. At the front, the couple cleared out overgrown hedges to create a large, sunny gravel auto court,

TOP *Old stone garden urns with carved fruit are set on wooden columns to create a framed entry to the dining room.*

ABOVE *A corner fireplace, its mantle displaying a collection of faience rabbits wearing waistcoats and playing musical instruments, is the focal point of the family room.*

FACING PAGE *A large French blue buffet cabinet with glass doors is filled with table ware, and French bistro chairs surround the long wood table in the breakfast room.*

and rerouted a longer driveway through a grove of olive trees. Bay and privet hedges were added, along with Italian cypresses, to complete a more formal arrival space.

Inside, they built walls to create more discrete rooms, typical of older, more traditional houses. They installed old stone fireplace mantles, wood beams, aged limestone flooring, and colored cement floor tiles. Lucinda Lester had apprenticed in San Francisco with her mother, Phyllis Lester, also a designer, and the two became partners, traveling frequently to France to purchase antiques for their clients. She says that her house is largely furnished with the flotsam and jetsam from that enterprise with her mother, and it has the eclectic look of classic antiques casually arranged with more rustic country pieces. Everything is comfortable and inviting, nothing is perfect, and the house has the feel of lived-in heirloom elegance.

Equally at home with the design of the landscaping, Lester wanted a European Mediterranean garden suitable to the house rather than merely an overgrown slope with scattered olive trees. The kidney-shaped pool was also an obstacle, but when she tried to talk her husband into replacing it with a rectangular one, he sensibly drew the line and said, Forget it. Lester decided instead to pull out all of the Arizona flagstone paving around the pool and put in plants up to the pool's edge, turning it into a "pond" in the middle of a large rectangular planter. This gave her the geometry she needed to create a more axial layout for the rest of the garden. From the pool, she planted a long allée of lavender extending to the back of the property, with a cross-axis at midpoint interconnecting parterres on either side that she terraced with low stone walls.

It is indeed a French garden. Along with olive trees, there are fruit trees—peach, plum, persimmon, orange, and lots of lemon—some in large terra cotta pots. Inspired by Nicole de Vésian's garden La Louve in the south of France, Lester used boxwood, varieties of pittosporum, and dwarf myrtle to create

topiary balls in varying shades of dark to light greens and dusty grays. Boxwood hedges define gray gravel paths, and lavender, rosemary, thyme and other herbs abound. Off the breakfast room is a pergola covered with a white rose vine, white wisteria, and a grape vine, each with its complementary seasonal changes. Off to one side are six fruitless mulberry trees making a leafy canopy of shade for a second summer dining area. From so inauspicious a starting point, the couple have fashioned a romantic French Eden.

TOP *A thick limestone table and old French garden chairs sit in the gravel terrace outside.*

ABOVE *A vine-covered trellis patio outside the breakfast room leads to a view of the long garden allée.*

RIGHT *A view of the pool, framed by surrounding clipped ball plantings, and the master bedroom wing beyond.*

FOLLOWING PAGES *The rear yard and pool from the master bedroom. A canopy of fruitless mulberry trees provide shade in summer and allow sun in the winter.*

CASA LEON

Palos Verdes Estates, 1929

PREVIOUS PAGES *Front approach to the house, featuring the central lawn and original clipped boxwood.*

RIGHT *A curving staircase leads to the garden room terrace and a spectacular ocean view.*

Part of the original Palos Verdes Estates developed by Frank A. Vanderlip (see Villa Narcissa, p. 72), Casa Leon (House of the Lion) was designed in 1929 by architect John P. Pederson for Margaret Keith, a daughter of the Keith–Orpheum Theaters family that founded RKO Pictures in 1929. The Olmstead Brothers were reportedly the original landscape designers for the property.

The Spanish Colonial house is approached from the road through dense, mature trees surrounding a central lawn, which is bordered by ball-shaped boxwood. The walled entry court, made smaller on account of high walls on three sides and the huge deodar cedar that crowds its center, gives no hint of the expansive vista one confronts upon entering through the front doors. Once inside, it is clear that this house enjoys a stunning hillside location with an ocean view that includes a long sweep of coastal cities extending westward to Santa Monica, Pacific Palisades, and Malibu beyond. Two stories tall on

ABOVE *Tiled risers and wrought-iron railing volutes add a bit of drama to the otherwise modest main stair.*

RIGHT *The entry hall includes arched openings, tile floors, wood beams, and other features typical of the Spanish Colonial Revival.*

the front, it is three-stories tall at the back, with a pool and garden terracing to a fourth and fifth level further down.

Doris and Mick Miguelez, the current owners who purchased the house in 1971 from aviator Frank Tallman, worked for a number of years on the interiors with Sandy Salmon, lead designer for Kasden's *La Tienda*. More recently, they have seamlessly added a new master bedroom suite, garden room, and terrace on the south side, with help from architect George Shaw from Edward Carson Beall & Associates. John Fleming, their interior designer since 1989 and, more recently, landscape designer Julie Heinsheimer have added their touches to the place. The paneled library remodeled by former owner and actor Paul Muni has been kept intact. It purportedly replicated a set from the movie *Louis Pasteur*, for which Muni won an Academy Award in 1935. A new elevator installed to facilitate up and down travel in this most vertical of houses also has surprise windows to the ocean at its stops.

It is clear that the Miguelezs and previous owners of this house have enjoyed its special setting, cultivating and safeguarding key parts of its history as they have remodeled and added on to accommodate changes. The power of the original design and details survive and even occasionally inspire improvements: Statues that stand on top of the walls at the pool, romantically silhouetted against the blue sea, were original to the house, but of such poor quality Doris and Mick replaced them in kind with the real thing from Florence!

TOP *An antique tiered stone fountain is a highlight of a side garden.*

ABOVE *A dramatic lion wall fountain presides in a small courtyard.*

RIGHT *Shadows enhance the delicate pattern of the entry court gates.*

ABOVE *The dining view terrace, protected on three sides, opens up on the fourth side to the breathtaking ocean view.*

RIGHT *A view of the house reveals its many levels and terraces.*

FOLLOWING PAGES *The spectacular "Queen's Necklace" of coastal cities as seen from the dining view terrace.*

VILLA ABBONDANZA

Los Angeles, 1923

PREVIOUS PAGES *A lush mix of climbing roses and Mediterranean plants at the street front give the house unusually friendly curb appeal.*

LEFT *The living room, which also opens to the front garden, contains a pink painted cupboard and blue painted chest, both by Beatrice Wood. The fireplace is a copy of one in the Palazzo Davanzati in Florence, Italy.*

ABOVE *The living room opens to a side loggia (left) and sunroom (right).*

This house on a modest lot in the Hancock Park area of Los Angeles acquired its tongue-in-cheek name not because of its size, but the abundant bounty its small but profusely planted gardens suggests to owners Roger and Cheryl Lerner. With their twin daughters and an army of pet cats, Roger, a physician, and Cheryl, a garden designer, enjoy the rich atmosphere of a small Italian country house, all packed into relatively tight quarters in an otherwise urban context.

The Lerners were lucky enough to have bought the house in 1986 from a couple who had owned the house for only two years after buying it in turn from the original owner, Mrs. Estelle K. Clemson. Clemson built the house in 1923 from plans designed by architect Marshall P. Wilkinson, Sr., and having divorced and then remarried her first husband, lived in the house for the next 60 years, apparently at one point enlisting Wilkinson's son, Marshall P. Wilkinson, Jr., to help remodel the

RIGHT *An American blue painted cupboard anchors one end of the sunroom, which is paved with a bold pattern of black and red tile.*

TOP *The dining room, with nineteenth-century American table, Windsor chairs, and an eighteenth-century painted cupboard from Pennsylvania.*

ABOVE *English hand-hammered copper cooking utensils and Vintage Bauer and Pacific Pottery are kitchen staples.*

AUTO
PAINTING
matisse

LEFT *A pencil post bed covered in vintage linens is the centerpiece of a child's bedroom.*

ABOVE *In a corner of the master bedroom, family photos covering a gate leg table, a Beatrice Wood drawing on the mantle, and a child's wicker rocker are just part of a lively tableau.*

master bedroom and one bathroom, perhaps in response to her "second" marriage.

The house the Lerners acquired, however, was not what one sees today: The narrow front yard was a barren lawn, and the small side and rear yards were relatively empty spaces disconnected from the house. They hired architects and landscape architects Tichenor & Thorp to help open up and transform the house and yard areas. They moved a fireplace in the living room, improving access to a loggia at the side, designed a trellised outdoor patio and fireplace at the rear, put in a pool on the other side yard, and developed a lushly planted garden along the front of the house.

Perhaps equally important, Brian Tichenor proposed a bold new color scheme for the exterior. When they repainted the dull, buff-colored house in brighter hues inspired by Tuscan villas, the Lerners raised a stir in the neighborhood, and were prevented from erecting a plaster wall at the front, which would have given them a more private outlook to the new garden. Twenty years later, however, it appears their vision has inspired other homeowners to be a bit

more adventurous in painting their houses.

Cheryl explains that on such a small lot, "the walls made it all work," and color "made it come alive." On the interior, she has chosen color schemes for the walls and moldings that have been inspired by Matisse on the one hand and Shaker traditions on the other. The hues are rich but subtle, and complement the family's lively collections of Americana and Beatrice Wood furniture pieces and drawings.

As a student, Cheryl spent time at the University of Pavia near Milan on a foreign study program, and there began her love affair with Italian culture and Mediterranean colors. Stepping into the Lerners' small backyard is like stepping into another room, where the attention to materials and details is just as intense as on the interior, with the added attraction of an array of plants in planters and numerous pots arranged around the furniture. This is where they do much of their entertaining, and where, with a little wine or Champagne and imagination thrown in, they and their guests can feel the touch of Italy gracing their lives. One has the same feeling strolling along the front path, where Rêve d'Or, Buff Beauty, and Mermaid rose varieties climb the front of the house and a heady mix of Mediterranean plantings fill the beds and tumble over the walkway. Elvin Garcia, who has faithfully tended the gardens since Cheryl put them in, is fastidious in maintaining the atmosphere she and Tichenor & Thorp created. "She's the brains, I'm the muscle," he says politely. Together they make a great team and have transformed the modest garden space into a lush and inviting paradise of *abbondanza*.

FACING PAGE *Vintage wrought-iron garden furniture sits under a pergola covered with* Petrea Volubis *in the rear yard.*

TOP *A view of the pergola from the courtyard and fireplace.*

ABOVE *Colorful printed pillows and cushioned lounge chairs surround the narrow side yard pool.*

VILLA DEI SOGNI

Palos Verdes, 1973

PREVIOUS PAGES *An ancient olive jar in a bed of flowers is the centerpiece to the entry court landing.*

ABOVE *The double-height entry features a trompe l'oeil fantasy surrounding the skylight.*

RIGHT *The owner's eclectic taste is revealed in the cozy living room. The painting above the fireplace is by Phillipe Auge.*

Villa dei Sogni (Villa of Dreams) in Palos Verdes was actually built in 1973, but it could easily have passed as part of the original Palos Verdes Estates started in 1912 by Frank A. Vanderlip and master-planned by the Olmstead Brothers. Some might even consider it to be a latter-day cousin to the Villa Narcissa (see p. 72).

The owners, an Italian–American family, hired local architect Edward Carson Beall to help them realize their dream house. They had long nurtured fond memories of Portofino, as well as several favorite villas in Tuscany and the Lake District of Lombardy. The layout of the house was influenced by the Hotel Splendido in Portofino, where all the rooms faced the sea. In their case, the view was of what is locally known as the "Queen's Necklace," the band of Los Angeles coastal cities that stretches northwest in an arc from Palos Verdes to Malibu. In a bold move, the owners painted the exterior a rich terra-cotta color appropriately reminiscent of some of their Italian counterparts, only to

PREVIOUS PAGES *The entry court loggia, complete with frescoed ceiling, is a fully furnished outdoor room.*

LEFT *Wall paintings on the outdoor shower are inspired by Pompeian frescos.*

BOTTOM LEFT *Sweeping views of the Santa Monica Bay and Los Angeles provide a dramatic background for alfresco dining on the stone tables.*

FACING PAGE *The rose garden entrance includes a wall plaque with the Latin inscription* Omnia Vincit Amor *(Love Conquers All).*

OMNIA
VINCIT
AMOR

ABOVE *Lion head fountains border a pergola where, on warm summer evenings, cocktails are often served, along with the 180-degree view.*

RIGHT *Windows and a continuous second floor loggia along the back of the house enjoy stunning views of the ocean.*

have the local authorities, who dictated a more muted palette of acceptable hues, slap a lien on their property.

For the interiors, they enlisted Beall's wife, Susie Beall, to help create an equally colorful yet comfortable arrangement of furniture and furnishings. The house has been a work-in-progress for over 30 years, remodeled regularly by the owners working with interior designer Peggy Braswell. At one point, an outdoor spa was installed (patterned after one at Pompeii), and on the occasion of a daughter's wedding, enormous murals were painted on the tennis court walls.

For the gardens, James Yoch was initially hired for some early landscape design work, but more recently local landscape designer Julie Heinsheimer has responded to the owners' desires that the landscape for their house be as equally inspired by Italian themes as the house. Heinsheimer created terraces, put in Italian cypresses, laid out rose gardens and built a pergola on the upper terrace. Off the kitchen, an herb garden was added, along with another pergola covered with grapevines. A profusion of broken stone columns, arches, urns, pots, and other garden ornaments decorate the grounds, while a mixture of gravel, stone and brick for the pathways and terraces suggest that different areas were added at different times in response to the vicissitudes of family life.

Villa dei Sogni is not a quiet, subtle affair, but a fun, nostalgically eclectic tribute that almost seems sunnier and more colorful than the Mediterranean architecture that was its inspiration.

CASA NUEVA

City of Industry, 1927

PREVIOUS PAGES *The entry courtyard and front façade.*

ABOVE *The* churrigueresque *hand-tooled and plaster front door surround has been masterfully restored by Bob Burchman and Ed Pinson.*

FACING PAGE *One of several stained glass windows found in the breakfast room.*

FOLLOWING PAGES *In the main hall, elaborate gessoed corbels, fine wrought-iron, decorative tiles, stained glass, and carved wood details create a rich atmosphere.*

During the tumultuous times of the Mexican–American war in mid-nineteenth-century California, Pio Pico, the last Mexican governor of Alta California, struggled to retain control of the state against the rising tide of U.S. immigration. Two of his friends and supporters, William Workman and indirectly his son-in-law F.P.F. Temple, were the beneficiaries of significant financial and real estate transactions arranged or sanctioned by Pico, including the acquisition of the 49,000-acre Rancho La Puente near Los Angeles. Their fortunes were not to endure. For the Temples, the failure of Workman's bank in 1876 signaled a period of financial ruin for the family that ultimately resulted in foreclosure of the Rancho property in 1899 and lasted until 1914, when oil was discovered on a small tract of land in the Montebello Hills, which Walter P. Temple, Temple's son, had purchased.

This temporary good fortune was enough to allow Temple and his wife Laura to repurchase 75 acres of his grandfather's property, including the original family homestead, in 1919. They also planned a new home for themselves next door called La Casa Nueva (The New House). Curiously, the first project Temple built on the property was a mausoleum designed after a classical temple to house the remains of his father and grandfather's families, as well as those of Pio Pico and his wife. In 1922, they hired the local architectural firm of Walker and Eisen to prepare plans for the new house. No sooner had construction begun, however, than Laura died, suspending the work for a time.

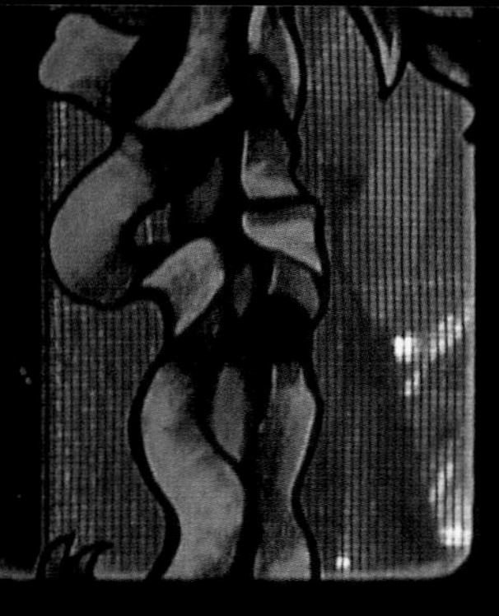

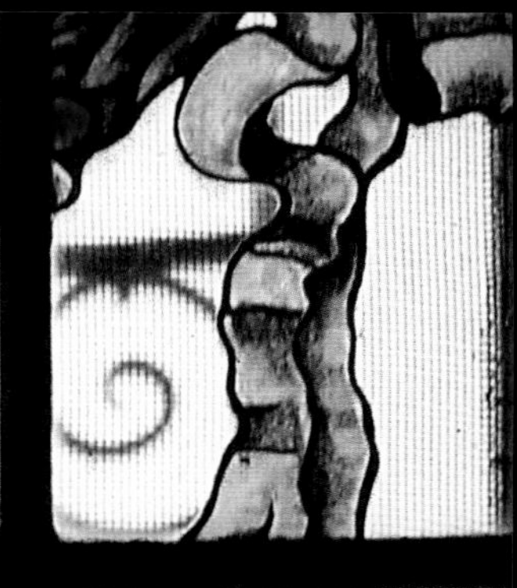

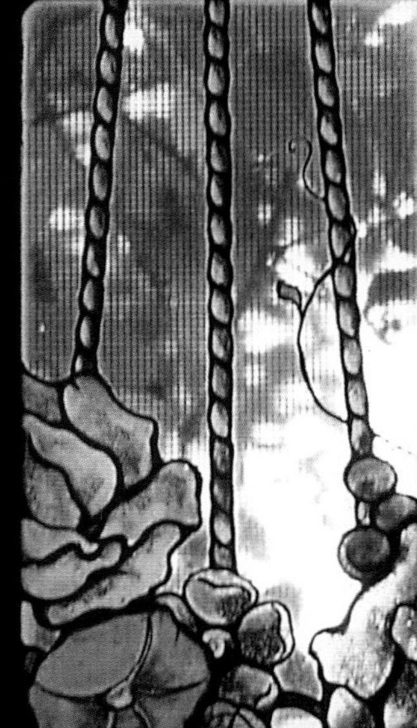

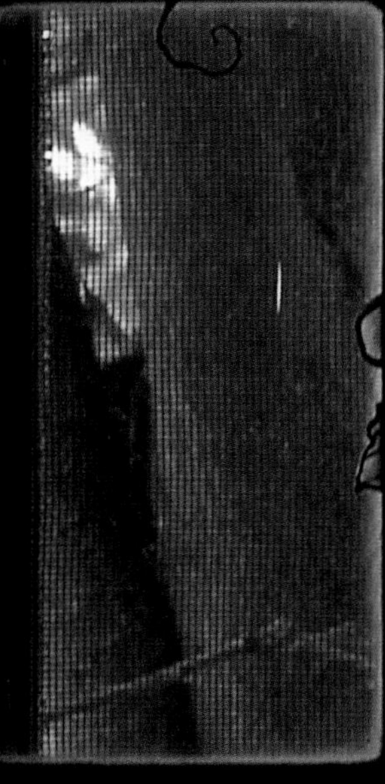

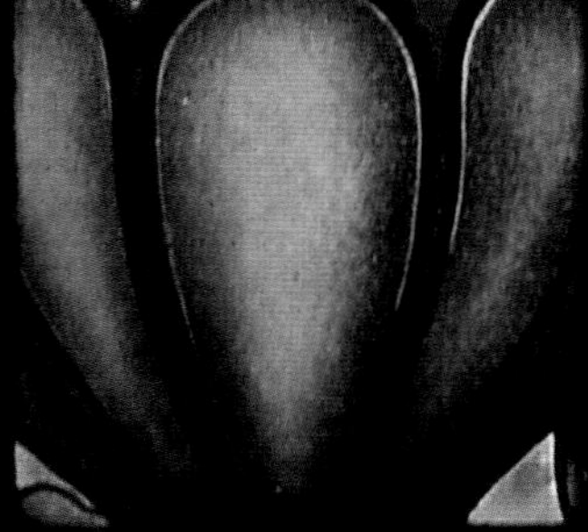
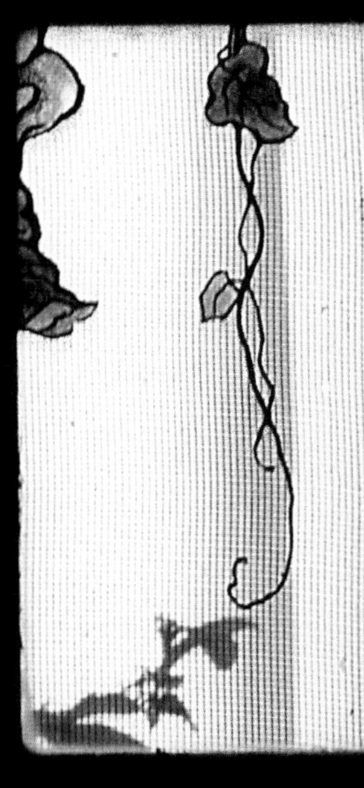
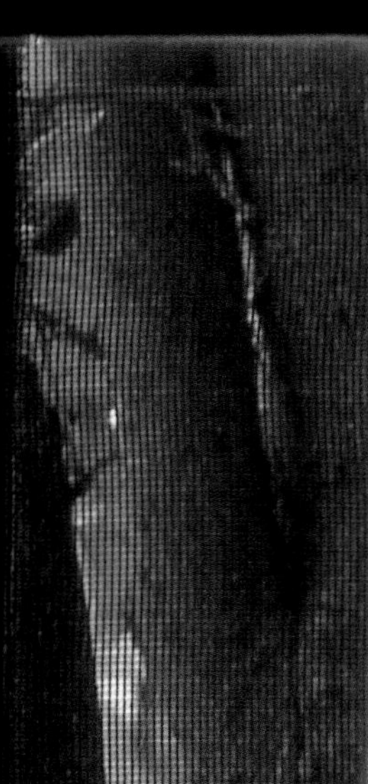
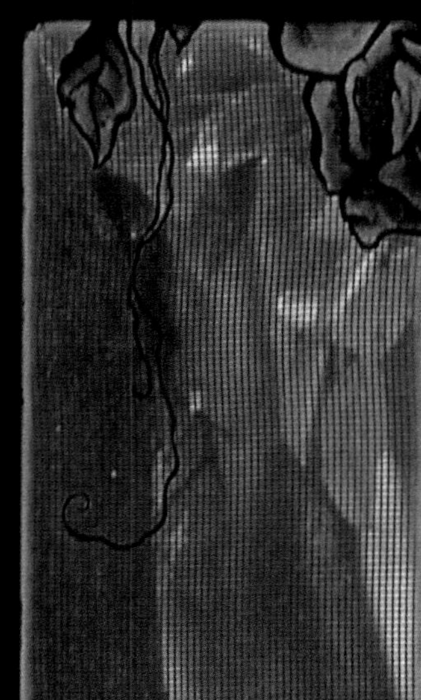

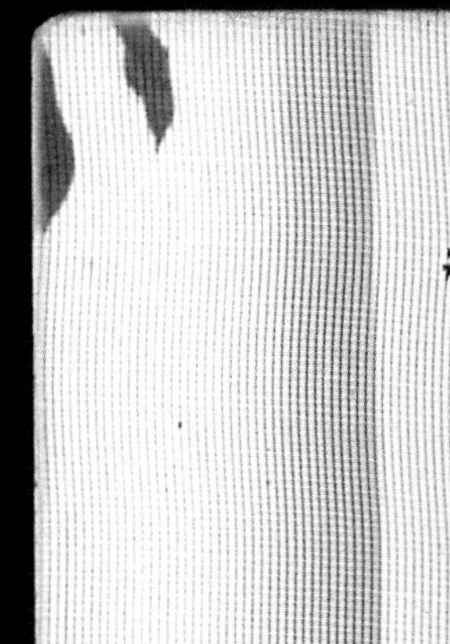

When construction resumed, a second architect, Roy Seldon Price, had taken over the supervision, and La Casa Nueva was finally completed in 1927. Temple's new financial success, however, was once again short-lived, and the failure of several of his oil prospecting and real estate development ventures led to the Temples' moving out in 1930 and the bank's foreclosing on the property in 1932.

Subsequently, the property was used as a boy's military school and then a convalescent hospital until the purchase by the City of Industry of the Cemetery and Workman's House in 1963 followed by La Casa Nueva in the early 1970s. Since then, it has received much deserved attention as the Workman and Temple Family Homestead Museum, and La Casa Nueva has been restored (by Raymond Girvigian and Mel Gooch), including its landscape (by Emmet Wemple and Associates), stained glass windows (by John Wallis), and tile restoration (by Goez Studios).

The Spanish Colonial two-story house is U-shaped in plan, an open porch surrounding a central courtyard on three sides. The entire house and its gardens are in turn surrounded by a perimeter wall and grapevine-covered pergola. The concrete paving in the pergola contains references to all of the California missions as well as decorative tiles depicting cattle brands. A grand front entry with an exuberant *churrigueresque* hand-tooled plaster surround, recently restored by decorative painters Bob Burchman and Ed Pinson, opens into the large, two-story high entrance stair hall with its second floor galleries leading to the upstairs bedrooms.

The interiors of the house are a treasure trove of period ceramic tile, woodwork, wrought-iron hardware, and stained glass. Much of the ceramic tile in the main hall, living room, dining room and library is from the town of Puebla, Mexico, and the tile panels were made by Pedro Sanchez, who worked for one of Puebla's companies. Floor tiles in the barbershop and breakfast room are compressed colored cement called "mosaico" frequently

TOP *The dining room, set with carved wood chairs, table, and sideboard.*

ABOVE *Stained glass irises in a breakfast room window recall the garden outside.*

FACING PAGE *Both American and Mexican tiles can be found throughout Casa Nueva.*

ABOVE *A whimsical rendition of Prince, the Temple family's dog, decorates the end of a beam light fixture.*

RIGHT *The central courtyard is surrounded on three sides by arcades on the ground floor and deep-set shaded windows above.*

used at the time in Spanish Colonial houses. American rather than Mexican tiles decorate the kitchen and bathrooms.

Much of the detailing of La Casa Nueva was intended to create the atmosphere of an old family Rancho that had evolved from a Spanish past. Family members depicted in the stained glass windows are set in period dress, a Spanish royal family coat of arms and a Temple family crest alternate with scenes of oil derricks, and the leading and glasswork were from the start made to look as if they had already been repaired from broken fragments. Perhaps this was a nostalgic remembrance of the family's former ties to Mexico, but it also may have been a self-conscious desire to hold on to a romanticized past in the face of the Temple family's uncertain financial situation and California's burgeoning industrial and political development during the 1920s. Today, the architecture of La Casa Nueva offers an intriguing glimpse into an important period of transition in California's cultural history.

La Casa Nueva and the other buildings comprising the Workman and Temple Family Homestead Museum are open to the public five days per week.

WOSK RESIDENCE AND STUDIO

Santa Monica, 1926/2001

PREVIOUS PAGES *The traditional Mediterranean Revival façade of the front of the house only hints at what's inside.*

ABOVE *The interior courtyard has a mosaic fireplace made of broken chards from the owner's mother's china, and 1940s childhood furniture from her childhood living room laden with memories.*

RIGHT *Like so many rooms in the house, the living room is a gallery, which includes a mosaic fireplace by Nancy Kin Tisch, a resin chandelier by Virgil Marti, and the owner's own art, among many other treasures.*

To enter Miriam Wosk's home and studio is to enter a domain where life and art are harmoniously and inextricably married. From the first step, one is stimulated by an amazing diversity of objects—furniture, furnishings, and art—that represent, in her words, "the archaeology of her soul and the visual diary of her travels, journeys, and experiences."

In 1981, at an earlier point in her career after first moving to Los Angeles from New York City, Wosk hired architect Frank Gehry to design a penthouse for her. It was an adventurously colorful apartment inspired perhaps by the move to Southern California's brighter climate. Twenty years later, however, Wosk wanted a change and moved closer to the ocean into an older 1926 Mediterranean Revival house with a yard.

In 2001, she hired architect Steven Ehrlich to help her remodel the house and add a painting studio. With assis-

HYGIENE

LEFT *The blue box sculpture on the table is by Lita Albiquerque. The chairs were painted by the owner.*

ABOVE *A bold display of flea market finds such as the pitchers, vintage Italian and American glassware, and cowhide covered stools make for unusual kitchen scenery.*

tance from interior designers Ellen Hoffman and Danna Vest, the project resulted in a paradoxical mix of modern and traditional that nevertheless seems to appropriately fit Wosk's creative environment.

While the front of the old house remains largely intact, the studio at the back is a distinctly contemporary addition. Its sliding pocket doors and skylights make it an indoor/outdoor space every bit as much, if not more than, a traditional porch or loggia might be. The addition was combined with an ambitious interior remodeling of the old house that gutted walls and opened up the interior spaces to each other and the exterior garden and pool. As a result, the line between inside and out has become much thinner, and an outdoor patio and fireplace seem to be as finished and decorated a setting as any of the interior rooms.

Pervading this mixed marriage of traditional and modern is Wosk's extraordinarily powerful appreciation of color. Mediterranean and Mexican in spirit, it seems to inspire everything from her own art to the things she collects to the walls that contain it all. The making of this place was clearly a very personal affair, and every square inch of it testifies to this labor of love.

Entering the library, where on a large central table new books are piled in order like place settings, is like entering a dining room where the table is festively set for some grand feast. Wosk says that rather than academia, the books she has bought have been her education, and their images inspire her art. The idea of collage—so central to her art—seems to be at the heart and soul of her home and personal life, as well. Indeed, her appetite for collecting seems

TOP *Brightly colored glazed pottery punctuates the deep purple, blues, and greens of the guesthouse pool and hedge.*

ABOVE *The guesthouse color pays homage to the studio of Mexican artist, Freida Khalo.*

RIGHT *Architect Stephen Ehrlich designed the studio addition, reflected here in the pool.*

insatiable, and nothing escapes her consideration. After the last major earthquake in Los Angeles, she carefully swept up and kept the shards of broken pottery and glass that most of us would have thrown away. She knew, she says, "they would make something beautiful someday, like the phoenix rising from the ashes." Today they adorn her outdoor fireplace and barbecue.

RANCHO LOS ALAMITOS

Long Beach, c. 1800

PREVIOUS PAGES *Two huge Moreton Bay fig trees tower over the front of the ranch house.*

ABOVE *The music room displays the Bixby's small but fine art collection; many pieces on display her are copies of originals bequeathed to museums.*

RIGHT *The library is part of the original adobe ranch house. All of the furniture, art, and books belonged to the owners.*

Perhaps more has been written about Rancho Los Alamitos (Ranch of the Little Cottonwoods) than any of the other properties included here, but it has had a long and involved history, spanning Native American settlements around 500 A.D. to the Spanish, Mexican, and American periods of California's past. From the late 1700s when an original 300,000 acres of land were granted to Manuel Nieto, it witnessed an incredibly turbulent changing of hands through the Figueroa, Stearns, Reese, and Bixby families. The last of these, the Bixbys, held ownership in one form or another through their own family's comings and goings from 1881 to 1967. In 1968, the Bixby heirs officially donated Rancho Los Alamitos to the City of Long Beach to be administered as a public historic site.

Needless to say, those original 300,000 acres, which had been reduced to 26,393 acres by the time John and Susan Bixby purchased the ranch in 1881, have today dwindled significantly to a relatively small parcel of 7.5 acres, consisting principally of the original homestead buildings and gardens. One now approaches the property via freeways and highways through a crowded and busy urban neighborhood of Long Beach. There is nothing left of the expansive open ranch land that was for so many decades its most salient feature. The small island of homestead buildings that remains hidden in this urban sea, however, still preserves the aura of the early-twentieth-century Bixby Rancho. When you finally arrive, the mature vegetation of the surrounding gardens allows you to forget what you just drove through getting there, and you start to see Rancho Los Alamitos as the place it once was.

One of the reasons for this is the restraint with which the gardens have been restored. They are still a little rough around the edges, as one would expect at a working family ranch, and executive director Pamela Seager and her staff have worked hard to let the gardens retain their original, rural character and avoid becoming institutionalized. One can appreciate that these gardens were both an oasis in the open land and a retreat from the busy life of the house and working ranch.

PREVIOUS PAGES *The billiard table is a Brunswick, purchased by John Bixby in the late nineteenth century as a gift to the YMCA, which apparently rejected it at the time for fear it would encourage bad habits in the young men.*

ABOVE *Two pelicans by Wella Potteries guard the gate from the back patio into the secret garden.*

RIGHT *In the Bixby era, the front porch offered a cool retreat from which to gaze out over the lawn to the tennis court and foothills beyond.*

The gardens owe most of their development initially to John Bixby's wife Susan, who beginning in 1873 lined the ranch roads with pepper trees and was responsible for planting the two Morton Bay fig trees in 1890 that now dominate the lawn east of the long loggia that connects the house to the garden on this side. Following John's and Susan's deaths in 1906, their son, Fred Bixby, and his wife Florence moved to the ranch, and it was Florence who for the next 30 years devoted herself to expanding and nurturing the gardens to their full maturity.

Florence hired numerous professional garden experts to assist her in this, including William Hertrich, Allen Chickering, Ed and Paul J. Howard, Yoch and Council, Charles Gibbs Adams, and most notably the Olmstead Brothers, but she maintained an active and dominant role in all the designs and plantings. As a result, there are suggestions here and there of a more formal European garden structure typical of many grand estates of the time, but they are clearly tempered by Florence's personal touches and appear to have happened in a less self-conscious way intermittently over time. Rather than strictly adhering to one single "grand scheme," different sections of the gardens appear to have been put in at different times for different reasons, so that the whole is more of a patchwork quilt than an ordered plan. This is a fitting consequence of having been a garden on a working ranch without the usual pretensions typical of most residential estates.

The main ranch house, too, was developed and expanded over time without the signature of any single initial architectural plan. From the original four-room adobe house (circa 1800), it gradually acquired additions as family needs arose, eventually taking on a rough but more formally organized U-shape around a central garden courtyard of lawn and palm trees. Like the gardens that surround it, it simply grew from humble beginnings, and reflects the ranch's long and rich history rather than any single occupation. It is this characteristic that distinguishes Rancho Los Alamitos and makes it a unique and valuable reference to Old California.

Rancho Los Alamitos is open to the public Wednesday through Sunday afternoons from 1:00 p.m. to 5:00 p.m.

LEFT *Designed by Florence Yoch around 1922, the Geranium Walk replaced an informal Shetland pony pasture.*

TOP *A corner of the secret garden, designed for Florence Bixby by the Olmstead Brothers in 1927.*

ABOVE *The Friendly Garden, also by Olmstead, was named for plants and cuttings planted there that were given to Florence Bixby by her friends.*

KIRBY RESIDENCE

Hollywood, 1926

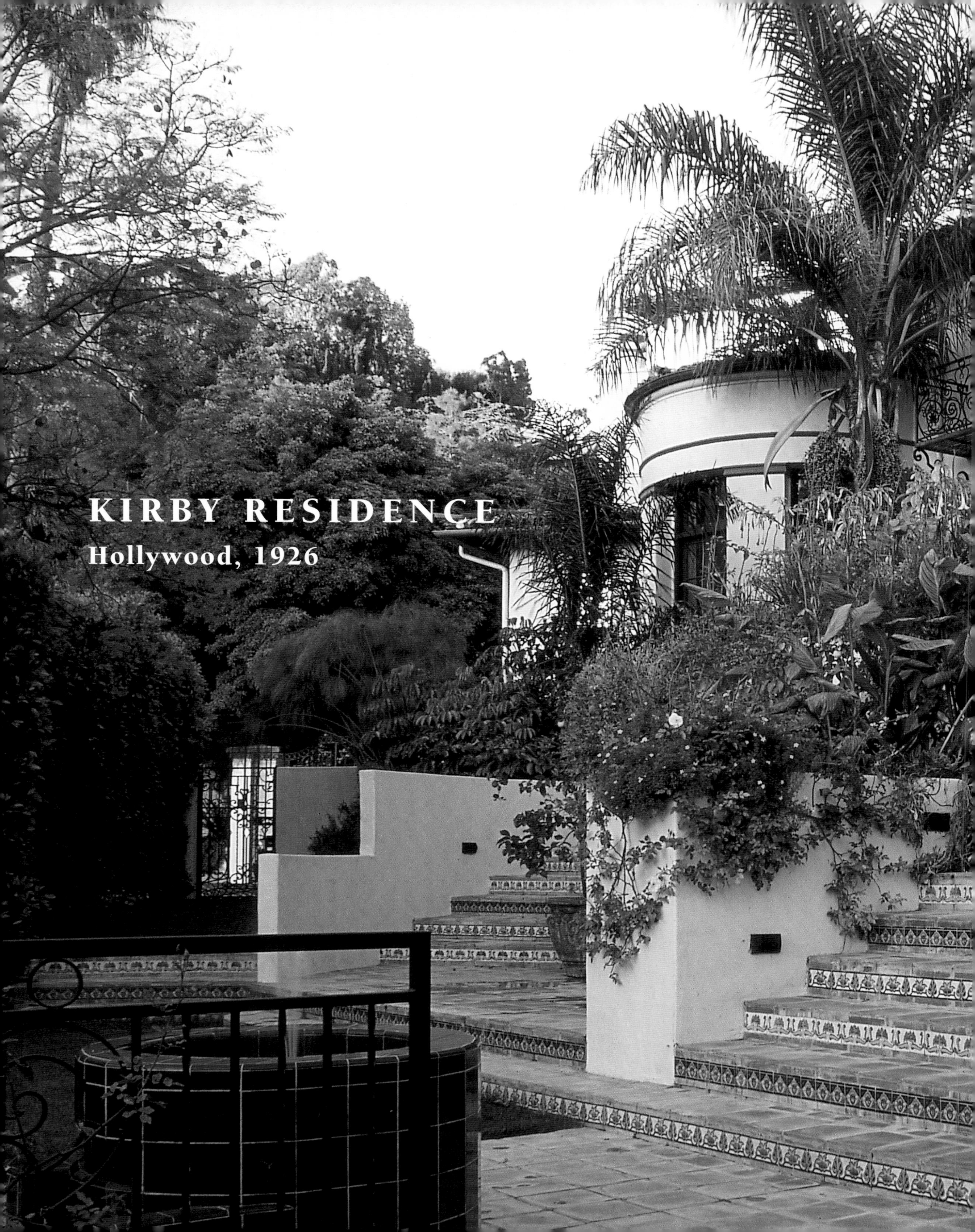

PREVIOUS PAGES *Grand steps, the equivalent of two stories, lead up to the front door from the street.*

ABOVE *A circular stair winds around the rotunda of the entrance hall.*

RIGHT *Decorative tile risers punctuate the stair treads.*

FACING PAGE *The entrance hall, looking into the dining room, with the landing above leading to upstairs bedrooms.*

FOLLOWING PAGES *The living room windows look out over the city on one side (not shown), and on the other to a rocky hillside garden and water feature.*

Old Hollywood is fertile territory for discovering 1920s-era Mediterranean and Spanish Colonial houses that in many instances exhibit more eccentric and quirky details than might normally be found in other examples of the stylistic vocabulary. Often, these houses had a history of being built or inhabited by famous (or not-so-famous) movie stars and perhaps the "industry" connections here often led the architecture in more theatrical directions.

This quirkiness is fairly descriptive of the Kirby Residence, which has recently been renovated by Jack Kirby with interior design by Steven Wilder, decorative painting by Bob Burchman and Ed Pinson, and landscaping by Rogerio

FACING PAGE *The dining room still retains its wrought-iron gates*

ABOVE *The upstairs bedrooms are small but sumptuously decorated.*

Carvalheiro and Brent Green. The renovation has added a number of contemporary elements, including a vibrantly colored, blue–tiled fountain at the front entry stair, to an already existing array of eclectic details, but also restored the original entry stair hall and loggia. Perched on an up-sloping corner lot, the house has a commanding view out over the city from its loggia and pool area, which offer a pleasant place to sit and recline outdoors on the sunny side of the house. On the uphill side off the kitchen, a small intimate courtyard and fountain carved into the hillside provides a private, shady retreat from the summer sun.

The original house was designed in 1926 by Marshall P. Wilkinson, Sr., for an ice cream king from Chicago and construction was completed in 1928. It was among the first houses built in Outpost Estates, one of the oldest residential neighborhoods in the foothills of Hollywood and the brainchild of developer Charles E. Toberman. The original lot was covered in pine trees, which Wilkinson apparently moved to his own property before construction began on the house.

A few blocks up from Grauman's Chinese Theater, the house does in fact have a history connected with Hollywood. It was briefly rented by the famous crooner, Russ Columbo, who at the time of his much-publicized and mysterious death was squiring Carole

ABOVE *The swimming pool is terraced into the hillside as an extension of the house.*

RIGHT *A south-facing loggia, connecting the house to the pool, looks out over the hillside to city views.*

Lombard around town. Columbo had met the recently divorced Lombard in 1933, and apparently moved to Outpost Estates to be near her home. In September 1934, two days after attending a sneak preview of one of his films with Lombard, Columbo was fatally shot at his best friend's home. Ruled accidental, the incident remains an only-in-Hollywood mystery.

Subsequently, from 1935 to the end of the century, the house was home to the family of film actor Alan Hale, Sr. His son, the television actor, Alan Hale, Jr., of *Gilligan's Island* fame, and daughter, Karen Hale Wookey, a script supervisor on *Heaven Can Wait*, *Patriot Games*, and other films, grew up in the house. According to Virginia Hall, an old friend of the Hale family and a frequent houseguest, the Hales were gracious hosts and had great pool parties, at which she and Karen often played two pianos together. It's a challenge looking at the relatively small size of the rooms imagining where two pianos might comfortably fit, but perhaps they were uprights.

YARIV RESIDENCE

Pasadena, 1924

PREVIOUS PAGES *The shaded rear courtyard of the residence faces north over the Arroyo Seco to the mountains beyond.*

ABOVE *A delicate but elegantly designed wrought-iron railing gracefully accents the stair.*

FACING PAGE *A large richly detailed Serapi Rug in the entry contrast with vaulted plaster ceiling.*

This Spanish Colonial Revival house and property has had numerous owners since 1924, the year it was designed by Joseph J. Kucera for its original owners, Mr. and Mrs. Harvey Bates and Mrs. Bates sister, Miss Emma Martindale. Originally it included the lots on either side, but over the years these were sold off, leaving the house and center lot. A former garage and chauffeur's apartment still survive on the adjacent lot to the north.

One of the most significant additions to the house property happened in 1929 when the new owner, Mr. Robert Campbell, hired landscape architect Charles G. Adams to develop the garden. No doubt inspired by Italian garden traditions, Campbell and Adams added retaining walls to create terraces, walkways, and rose-cutting gardens. By the time Amnon and Fran Yariv purchased the property in 2001, however, the garden had evolved into a hodgepodge of inappropriate plantings obscuring Adams's original plan.

The house, on the other hand, was in remarkably good shape, and with assistance from local interior designer Pat McNamara, the Yarivs completed a renovation started by the previous owner, making a few of their own changes. Situated along a bank overlooking the Arroyo Seco, the house's main terrace must have once enjoyed splendid mountain views towards the east, now largely blocked by the growth of mature oak trees on this side. To the west, a smaller enclosed courtyard opening off a glassed-in loggia offers a sunny prospect and an invitation to dine outside.

The larger surrounding gardens to the south and west were a challenge successfully met by the Yariv's daughter, landscape designer Gabriela Yariv. Inspired by the Mediterranean garden traditions both locally and abroad, Gabriela recreated the rectangular lawn, restored the classic

PREVIOUS PAGES *The living room is simply furnished in a neutral palette and clean lines.*

TOP *An arched wrought-iron gate leads to the pool area.*

ABOVE *The lower garden was designed by the owner's daughter to include drought-tolerant plants typical of Mediterranean gardens.*

RIGHT *A gallery opens out to the enclosed west patio with its large ceramic pot fountain.*

axial order to the garden, and revived a more suitably drought-tolerant plant palette that included olive trees, Italian cypress, succulents, and cacti, as well as sage, verbena, rosemary, and other varieties. Against the strong formal structure of the original layout of terraces, walls, stairs, stone balustrades, and fountains, her new plantings are layered and varied, giving a softer, more informal and slightly overgrown character to house and property reminiscent of a venerable European country villa.

ARCADY PAVILION

Montecito, 1920s/1953

The former music pavilion at Arcady, the Santa Barbara estate developed by George Owen Knapp at the beginning of the twentieth century, was originally an underground ballroom with an open terrace for its roof. The ballroom, which was dug into the top of the north crest of a hill facing the Santa Ynez Mountains, was one of several outbuildings that populated the estate's gardens. Surrounded by eucalyptus trees and with magnificent views from the crest of the hill, the original terrace must have seemed like a romantic scene from a Maxfield Parish painting.

Knapp, who had been a successful civil engineer, parlayed his interests in gas and electricity into an empire that would eventually become Union Carbide. In 1911, he purchased 70 acres and a house (a property which eventually grew to almost 200 acres) from Ralph Radcliffe Whitehead, an English expatriate who had settled in Santa Barbara in 1894. He not only ambitiously added on to the Tuscan-style main house with help from architect E. Russell Ray, but also developed 50 acres of gardens. Francis T. Underhill designed the lower gardens and Carleton M. Winslow designed the upper gardens. The ballroom, constructed as part of the "Green Garden," was just one of a number of structures such as guest cottages, stables, a pool and pool house that were built in the 1920s throughout the estate's extensive gardens to complement their lifestyle as grand entertainers and civic leaders. In 1926, the estate was one of several celebrated by The Garden Club of America on its first official tour of California gardens.

Like many grand estates following the Depression, Arcady—which was willed to Knapp's son in 1938—fell on hard

PREVIOUS PAGES *Arcady Pavilion and its grand garden stair against the mountains. The eucalyptus trees, Champagne fountain, and covered stone are all original to the Estate*

ABOVE *An eighteenth-century bust of Emperor Augustus and two second-century Roman heads of women preside over the living room furniture.*

FACING PAGE *A carved giltwood Italian mirror dominates the wall above the nineteenth-century Italian stone mantle, flanked by double-height windows.*

times and was sold in 1941. It was subsequently subdivided into different parcels, the ballroom and a portion of the upper garden being one. In 1953, a new owner, Mrs. James Hayes, commissioned Mary Craig to design a three-bedroom, one-story house, which they placed on the ballroom's roof terrace. Under the subsequent ownership of Charles A. Rheinstrom during the 1960s, the landscape architect W. Bennet Covert added a swimming pool and tennis court.

LEFT *The terrace off the dining room looks into dense planting of oak and olive trees. The chairs are eighteenth-century Italian Neoclassical.*

ABOVE *The downstairs loggia, the estate's original music pavilion, opens at each end to the house into the side gardens.*

Behind a large stone fountain, a Neoclassical pediment by architect Jack Warner frames the glass front entry doors.

More recently, the current owners, Alice Willfong and her late husband Donald, guided by their friend and business partner, interior designer Craig Wright, remodeled the house with architect Jack Warner, putting in a new stair to the former ballroom below, adding guestrooms and creating a lighter, more livable and grander setting for their collection of Roman antiquities and antiques. Alice tells her guests that the new stair, which involved significant costs to push out the foundation, "is the most expensive stairway they will ever descend."

The former downstairs ballroom, its mountain views now partially blocked by mature oak trees, was opened up laterally to reconnect it to side gardens. In order to do this, the Willfongs bought several pieces of adjacent properties to extend the axes. The new classical entrance portico Warner added at the upper level gives it an appropriate scale and formality that ceremoniously connect it to the grand fountain and stairs

TOP *A large terrace in the western garden provides a fitting arena for scattered carved stone fragments, sculptures, and Italian terra cotta jars.*

ABOVE *The swimming pool is flanked by Italian olive jars.*

RIGHT *A view from the west of the downstairs loggia, with living room and terrace above.*

from the sunken garden that were parts of the original Green Garden. The surrounding landscape has also been revitalized with help from landscape architect Sydney Baumgartner, and it is now easy to forget that this was just part of a much larger subdivided estate and appreciate how wonderfully integrated and special a place it has become on its own. It is perhaps a lesson that the garden, even a piece of one, can often inspire the creation of a house, rather than the other way around.

CASA DE LAS CAMPANAS

Los Angeles, 1928

350

PREVIOUS PAGES *The street façade of the house offers an extended wall of delightfully asymmetrical rooflines, doors, windows, balconies, and other features.*

ABOVE *The elaborately carved wood entrance door and frame are boldly recessed into the larger stone archway.*

FACING PAGE *The bell tower includes a four-bell carillon driven by 1907 E. Howard (Boston) clockworks. The stained glass window below is by Tiffany Studios.*

Willis Howard Mead and his wife Irene paid $50,000 for two lots adjacent to the new Wilshire Country Club in Hancock Park. In the Los Angeles of the early 1920s and even given the high-end location, this was a steep price tag. Mead, one of the owners of a major Los Angeles building supply company, was no doubt riding high at the time on profits from a business closely tied to Los Angeles's burgeoning urban growth.

In 1926, after several abortive attempts at plans with other architects, the Meads hired a relatively young but talented architect named Lester G. Scherer to design their new home. Scherer's predicament was that he was obliged to work with the ideas and suggestions of the Meads' energetic daughter, Lucile Mead. It appears that both architect and client nevertheless survived the ordeal admirably, and the house was completed in 1928.

Whether thanks to Scherer's skill or Lucile Mead's vision, La Casa de las Campanas (The House of the Bells) is a wonderfully expansive work of architecture. Inspired by Andalusian precedents but decorated with elements more reminiscent of the Spanish Renaissance, the exterior is an impressive exercise in asymmetrical composition. Its long, flat entrance façade sits squarely facing the street and the central *Plateresco*-style stone entrance archway presents a ceremoniously formal statement. Within this solid plane of the façade, however, is a riot of different windows, chimneys, balconies, and broken rooflines that adds a more playful note to the proceedings.

Upon entering the house, an even richer mix of influences continues to take one by surprise at every turn. To the right of the entry is a beautifully proportioned, two-story-high living room with corbelled trusses and beams supporting a

ABOVE *Floral painted arches above the door and window openings decorate an informal dining area.*

RIGHT *A corner sunroom leads to a tiled archway to the billiard room beyond.*

FOLLOWING PAGES *Above the fireplace in the billiard room is a triptych by Marion Wachtel. The table is a 1991 Brunswick quarter-swam Oak Pot Belly model.*

hand-carved and painted wood ceiling. At the far end, an off-center tiled stair climbs to a balcony over a large central, semi-circular archway. Here, the basic symmetry of the whole is delightfully interrupted by the asymmetrical placement of the stair and its thick plaster railing wall. To the left of the entry is an octagonal stair hall with its stair climbing around the perimeter, each side of the octagon offering something different, including a built-in organ. Here, the screen covering the organ pipes, the stained glass ceiling, the stair railing, and other details are distinctly Art Deco. Instead of smooth walls, these plaster walls are intricately textured and colored to simulate a travertine veneer. This is definitely not an orthodox Spanish interior.

Elsewhere inserted in the design of the house are presumably incongruous Victorian elements. The entire walnut-paneled dining room was salvaged from a large Victorian house demolished in

TOP *The Victorian-era iron conservatory was salvaged from another property and removed to its present location in 1927. The windows are attributed to Tiffany Studios.*

ABOVE *An elaborately tiled tub in the bathroom is flanked by recesses for shower and water closet.*

FACING PAGE TOP *The shape of the colorful tile-work fountain at the end of the pool is mimicked by the Mission-style wall behind.*

FACING PAGE BOTTOM *A fountain dominates one of the rear side gardens.*

1924, along with numerous fixtures and a complete glass and lath conservancy, which was attached like a caboose to the rear of the house. These and other eclectic finishes and decorations were likely due to Lucile Mead's youthfully creative enthusiasm and represent an intentionally diverting confusion of styles that would seem more jarring and out of place if they were not so beautifully crafted and contained within the confidently designed and consistently robust Spanish Colonial exterior. The plan of the house, organized easily around two courtyards, and the playful sculptural massing of the architecture, including the bell tower that gives the house its name, are strong enough to hold this decorative interior turmoil together.

Lucile Mead survived her parents and continued to live in the house until her death in 1985. Television and movie producers Leonard Hill and Ann Daniel were the lucky buyers a year later of a house and furnishings that had remained essentially intact since 1928, but by then the place was a bit overgrown and worn and had accumulated over half a century of dirt and grime. With assistance from architects Milofsky and Michali, Tom Cox for landscaping, and Rich Assenberg on the interiors, they attentively restored the house, remodeled the master suite and kitchen, transformed the landscaping, and added a pool and outdoor fireplace off the rear courtyard.

Hill has combined his own fine collections of furniture, paintings, pottery, and Spanish colonial carvings, all of which seem in keeping with the delightfully eclectic mixture of styles and decoration that gave the original house its unique character. He has also edited a wonderful documentary film, using original footage of the house's construction from the Meads' film archives, which not only tells the house's story but also confirms Hill's passionate dedication to the restoration of what is now an official Los Angeles Cultural Heritage Monument.

ILLA DILEMMA

nta Barbara, 1930

Restoration and interiors by John Saladino.

Restoration and interiors by John Saladino.

PREVIOUS PAGES *The Pompeian atrium is a contained outdoor room largely planted with scented flowers. Heliotrope, datura, and jasmine soften the rectangular geometry of the space.*

ABOVE *The dining room is carried out in white, platinum, ice blue, and iridescent periwinkle. An over-scaled eighteenth-century candle chandelier compliments the round table.*

RIGHT *With its great proportions and high fireplace, the largest room in the house, the living room, is remarkably comfortable.*

When 14-year-old John Saladino first visited Santa Barbara with his parents, he knew that someday he would return there to live. It took awhile, but on a trip there in 1985 with his late wife, he saw a dilapidated stone farmhouse on 12.5 acres that looked like something plucked out of the Italian countryside. He waited until 2001 to finally buy it, and then he really began to realize the challenge he and his partner, Betty Barrett, had accepted.

The house was a ruin, with a host of both architectural and structural problems that had been exacerbated over the years by deferred maintenance and abusive tenants. By the 1950s, most of the original finish surfaces had either been removed or covered over. It took six men an entire year to strip peach-colored paint off all the stone walls and beams. At one point, someone had installed acoustic tile over the original ceilings and, at another, polished red granite tiles over the original stone and terra cotta floors. The stone stairs had been ripped out and would all have to be painstakingly remade by hand. Major remedial foundation work was mandated and reinforcing added. New exterior windows and doors were installed throughout.

The original house was designed in 1929 by architect Wallace Frost for himself. Frost was what early Californians referred to as "an East Coast architect," in this case from Detroit, where he apparently had designed an office building for the Ford Family. A great Italophile, Frost felt that California and its sunshine called to him, perhaps as much as they spoke to Saladino years later. He was intent on building a house

Restoration and interiors by John Saladino.

Restoration and interiors by John Saladino.

ABOVE *The breakfast room's elegant steel door gives access to the large south terraces, the villa's major outdoor entertainment space.*

RIGHT *A view of the motor court from the porte-cochere. The blue/gray color theme of the garden is continued with lavender and blue agaves.*

for himself that would reflect his fondest dreams, and he did, even employing Italian workers to execute it. Sandstone quarried on site was used for the walls and local clay for the tile floors. It was an Italian farmhouse made of vernacular Santa Barbara materials by Italians. Although Frost lived in his new home through the Depression, it appears that he found no work in California to sustain his practice and was forced to move back east.

"This was the *most* difficult restoration of my career," Saladino states in his inimitable way. One of the things that apparently made the house so appealingly quirky was also what made the restoration so complicated. Nothing lined up or was truly square, not a single dimension was repeated, and as a result every bit of new work had to be custom fitted. Saladino's explanation as to why the house may have been so out of whack seems quite plausible, that Frost had drawn up rudimentary plans dimensioned in feet and inches, but his Italian workers converted everything to approximate metric equivalents with the result that nothing fit perfectly, no doubt adding to the Villa's charm.

Although the restoration was a grueling four and a half year experience, one has the feeling that Saladino knew what he had all along and saw light at the end of the tunnel. He appreciated Frost's original visionary planning—that he had respected the site, building into the side of the hill rather than dominating the top of it, that he had nestled the house discreetly into a forest of eucalyptus trees, but managed to take advantage of ocean and mountain views. Saladino also respected the basic architecture of Frost's building, stripping away the later tenant additions and desecrations that violated the house, but keeping the essential original elements, even when they were broken or worn.

What is truly remarkable, however, is how skillfully and sensitively Saladino enhanced the original house, turning the home into something that has become as

Restoration and interiors by John Saladino.

Restoration and interiors by John Saladino.

ABOVE *Ancient olive trees on the south terrace shade a table for Sunday family luncheons.*

RIGHT *The agave terrace to the left is the high point in the garden, and overlooks the swimming pool and pergola.*

much comfortable villa as farmhouse and giving it a landscaped setting equal to the architecture. He planted hundreds of new trees and plants and developed garden, court, and terrace areas around the house that extend it outside. The grand entry court, the gravel dining terrace amid olive trees, the inner Pompeian courtyard of scented plants climbing gloriously up the hill behind, and the dramatic terraced pool area that looks westward over the treetops towards the Pacific Ocean and setting sun beyond—these are all rich improvements by a masterful hand. Not content to stop there, he reached further out into the site, lining the ascending driveway with old Italian Cypress trees to add ceremony to one's arrival and weaving a ribbon of blue ice plants through the eucalyptus grove to create an idealized stream through the forest.

On the interior, without changing Frost's stone shell, Saladino carefully refined and warmed it, playing carefully chosen artwork, furniture, tapestries and fabric off against the new rustic patina of floors, walls and ceilings. Somehow, the old farmhouse was made to seem even older in the process, but elegantly so. The pigs and chickens are no longer running around the house, just the Count and Countess now, but the memory of the farm still lingers, making this the most unpretentious of villas.

Saladino claims that, "making this villa was a will to Paradise." It was clearly hard work, but his unique talent is that he made the end result look so easy. No designer practicing today does it better. Out of ruins he has created classically timeless magic.

Restoration and interiors by John Saladino.

SELECTIVE BIBLIOGRAPHY

Allen, Harris. "Spanish Atmosphere." *Pacific Coast Architect* 29 (May 1926): 5–33.

Ames, Meriam, et al, eds. *Rancho Santa Fe: A California Village*. Rancho Santa Fe, California: The Rancho Santa Fe Historical Society, 1993.

Amicis, Edmondo De. *Spain and the Spaniards*. 2 vols. Philadelphia: Henry T. Coates & Co., 1895.

Andree, Herb, Noel Young and Wayne McCall. *Santa Barbara Architecture: From Spanish Colonial to Modern*. Santa Barbara, California: Capra Press, 1975.

Appleton, Marc. *George Washington Smith: An Architect's Scrapbook*. Santa Monica, California: Tailwater Press, LLC, 2001.

Baldon, Cleo and Ib Melchior. *Reflections on the Pool: California Designs for Swimming*. New York: Rizzoli, 1997.

Bailley, Vernon Howe. *Little Known Towns of Spain*. New York: William Helburn Inc., 1927.

Belloli, Jay, et al. Wallace Neff 1895–1982: *The Romance of Regional Architecture*. San Marino, California: The Huntington Library, 1989.

——. *Johnson, Kaufmann, Coate: Partners in the California Style*. Claremont, California: Scripps–Capra Press, 1992.

Bissell, Ervanna Bowen. *Glimpses of Santa Barbara and Montecito Gardens*. Santa Barbara,California: 1926.

Boston Architectural Club (Frederic V. Little, Executive Secretary). *The Book of the Boston Architectural Club for 1925: Spain*. Boston: Boston Architectural Club Inc., 1926.

Bottomley, William Lawrence. *Spanish Details*. New York: William Helburn Inc., 1924.

Byne, Arthur and Mildred Stapley. *Rejeria of the Spanish Renaissance*. New York: The Hispanic Society of America, 1914.

——. *Spanish Ironwork*. New York: The Hispanic Society of America, 1915.

——. *Decorated Wooden Ceilings in Spain*. Manual. New York: G.P. Putnam's Sons, 1920.

——. *Decorated Wooden Ceilings in Spain*. Portfolio of Plates. New York: G.P. Putnam's Sons, 1920.

——. *Spanish Gardens and Patios*. Philadelphia: J.B. Lippincott Company, 1924.

——. *Provincial Houses in Spain*. New York. William Helburn Inc., 1925.

——. *Spanish Interiors and Furniture*. Vol. 3. New York: William Helburn Inc., 1925.

——. *Majorcan Houses and Gardens*. New York: William Helburn Inc., 1928.

Byne, Mildred Stapley. *Forgotten Shrines of Spain*. Philadelphia: J.B. Lippincott Company, 1926.

Cheney, Sheldon. *The New World Architecture*. 1930. New York: Longmans, Green & Company, 1930.

Clark, Alson. "*The 'Californian' Architecture of Gordon B. Kaufman*." Review. *Society of Architectural Historians Southern California Chapter* Vol. 1, No. 3 (Summer, 1982): 2.

Close, Bernard Wells, ed. *American Country Houses of Today: Small Houses, Bungalows, Etc*. New York: Architectural Book Publishing Co., 1922.

—— *American Country Houses of Today*. New York: Architectural Book Company, 1927.

Conard, Rebecca and Christopher H. Nelson. *Santa Barbara: A Guide to El Pueblo Viejo*. Santa Barbara, California: The City of Santa Barbara, 1986.

Cook, III, S. F. and Tim Skinner. *Spanish Revival Architecture*. Atglen, Pennsylvania: Schiffer Publishing, Ltd., 2005.

Curl, Donald W. *Mizner's Florida*. New York: The Architectural History Foundation and the MIT Press, 1984.

Dardick, Karen and Melba Levick. *Estate Gardens of California*. New York: Rizzoli Publishing International, 2002.

Davis, Walter S., et al. *California Garden City Homes: A Book of Stock Plans*. Los Angeles: Garden City Company of California, 1915. Rev. ed. 1946 as *Ideal Homes in Garden Communities: A Book of House Plans*.

De Forest, Elizabeth. "Old Santa Barbara Gardens and How They Came to Be." *Pacific Horticulture* 38 (Winter 1977–78): 31–36.

De Fries, H., ed. *Moderne Villen und Landhäusen*. Berlin: Ernst Wasmuth, 1924.

Dobyns, Winifred Starr. *California Gardens*. New York: MacMillan Company, 1931.

Eberlein, Harold Donaldson. *Villas of Florence and Tuscany*. Philadelphia: J.B. Lippincott Company, 1922.

——. *Spanish Interiors*. New York: Architectural Book Publishing Co., 1925.

Edgell, G.H. *The American Architecture of Today*. New York: Charles Scribner's Sons, 1928.

Embury, Amyar II. *One Hundred Country Houses, Modern American Examples*. New York: Century Company, 1909.

Feduchi, Luis. *Spanish Folk Architecture: The Northern Plateau*. Barcelona, Spain: Editorial Blume, 1974.

Fox, Helen Morgenthau. *Patio Gardens*. New York: MacMillan ompany, 1929.

Garnett, Porter. *Stately Homes of California*. Boston: Little, Brown and Company, 1915.

Garrison, Richard and George Rustay. *Mexican Houses*. New York: Architectural Book Publishing Co., 1930.

Gebhard, David. *George Washington Smith*, 1876–1930: *The Spanish Colonial Revival In California*. Exhibition Catalogue. Santa Barbara, California: UCSB Art Gallery, 1964.

——. "The Spanish Colonial Revival in Southern California (1895–1930)." *The Journal of the Society of Architectural Historians* 26 (1967): 131–147.

—— and Robert Winter. *A Guide to Architecture in Los Angeles and Southern California*. Santa Barbara and Salt Lake City: Peregrine Smith Inc., 1977.

—— and Harriette Von Breton. *Architecture in California, 1868–1968*. Exhibition Catalogue. Santa Barbara, California: The Art Galleries, UCSB, 1968.

——. "Architectural Imagery, the Mission and California." *The Harvard Architecture Review: Beyond the Modern Movement*. Cambridge: The MIT Press, Vol. 1, Spring 1980.

——. *Santa Barbara—The Creation of a New Spain in America*. Exhibition Catalogue. Santa Barbara, California: University Art Museum, 1982.

——, David Bricker and Lauren Weiss Bricker. A Catalogue of the Architectural Drawing Collection. Santa Barbara, California: The University Art Museum, UCSB, 1983.

—— ed. Myron Hunt, 1868–1952: *The Search for A Regional Architecture*. Santa Monica, California: Hennessey & Ingalls, Inc., 1984.

—— and Sheila Lynds, eds. *An Arcadian Landscape: The California Gardens of A.E. Hanson 1920–1932*. Los Angeles: Hennessey & Ingalls, Inc. 1985.

——. "Casa Del Herrero, the George F. Steedman House, Montecito, California." *Antiques* (August 1986).

——. "Founding Father: GWS." *Santa Barbara Magazine*. (July/August 1993).

——. *Lutah Maria Riggs*. Santa Barbara: Capra Press, 1992.

—— and Robert Winter. *Los Angeles: An Architectural Guide*. New York: Gibbs–Smith Publishers, 1994.
Gellner, Arrol and Douglas Keister. Red Tile Style: *America's Spanish Revival Architecture*. China: Viking Studio, 2002.
Gleye, Paul. *The Architecture of Los Angeles*. Los Angeles: Rosebud–Knapp, 1981.
Goodhue, Bertram Grosvenor. *Mexican Memories: The Record of a Slight Sojurn Below the Yellow Rio Grande*. New York: G. M. Allen Co., 1892.
Grey, Elmer. "Southern California Architecture" and an article in the *Southern California Home*. Privately published. Los Angeles: 1925.
Hannaford, Donald and Revel Edwards. *Spanish Colonial and Adobe Architecture of California, 1800–1850*. New York: Architectural Book Publishing Co., 1931.
Hanson, A.E. *An Arcadian Landscape*. Los Angeles: Hennessey & Ingalls, 1985.
Hewitt, Mark Alan. *The Architect & The American Country House 1890–1940*. New Haven: Yale University Press, 1990. pp. 42, 207–221, 282, 286.
Hielscher, Kurt. *Picturesque Spain*. New York: Brentano's, 1922.
Hitchcock, Henry Russell. *Modern Architecture: Romanticism and Reintegration*. New York: Payson and Clarke, Ltd., 1929.
Hunter, Paul R., and Walter L. Reichardt. *Residential Architecture in Southern California*. Los Angeles: Southern California Chapter, A.I.A., 1939.
Jackson, Helen Hunt. *Ramona*. Boston: Roberts Brothers, 1884.
Johnston, Alva. *The Legendary Mizners*. New York: Farrar, Straus & Young, 1953.
Johnston, Shirley and Roberto Schezen. *Palm Beach Houses*. New York: Rizzoli, 1991.
Kaplan, Sam Hall. *LA Lost & Found: An Architectural History of Los Angeles*. New York: Crown Publishers Inc., 1987.
Keefe, Charles S., ed. *The American House*. New York: U.P.C. Book Company Inc., 1922.
Kirker, Harold. *California's Architectural Frontier.* 3rd ed. Santa Barbara and Salt Lake City: Gibbs M. Smith, 1986.
——. *Old Forms on a New Land, California Architecture in Perspective*. Colorado: Roberts Rinehart Publishers, 1991.
Kowalczyk, Georg and Gustavo Gili, ed. *Hierros Artisticos*. Barcelona, Spain: 1927.
Lane, Jonathan. "The Period House in the Nineteen–Twenties." *Journal of the Society of Architectural Historians* 20 (1961): 169¬–178.
Lavender, David. *Historical Narrative: "Rancho Los Alamitos."* Rancho Los Alamitos Foundation. [No Date]
Lockwood, Charles and Jeff Hyland. *The Estates of Beverly Hills*. Beverly Hills, California: Margrant Publishing Co., 1984.
Lowell, Guy. *More Small Italian Villas and Farmhouses*. Architectural Book Publishing Co., 1920.
——. *Smaller Italian Villas and Farmhouses*. Vols. 1 and 2. New York: Architectural Book Publishing Co., 1922.
Mack, Gerstle and Thomas Gibson. *Architectural Details of Northern and Central Spain*. New York: William Helburn Inc., 1928.
——. *Architectural Details of Southern Spain*. New York: William Helburn Inc., 1928.
Major, Howard. *Palm Beach Villas*. Palm Beach: R.O. Davies Publishing Co., 1929.
Masson, Kathryn and James Chen. *Santa Barbara Style*. New York: Rizzoli Publishing International, 2001.
Mayer, August L. *Alt–Spanien*. New York: Architectural Book Publishing Co., 1920.
——. *Architecture and Applied Arts of Old Spain*. New York: Brentano's, 1921.
McClug, William Alexander. *Landscapes of Desire: Anglo Mythologies of Los Angeles*. Berkeley: University of California Press, 2000.
McCoy, Esther. *Five California Architects*. New York: Reinhold Book Corporation, 1960.
McGrew, Patrick. *Landmarks of Los Angeles*. New York: Harry N. Abrams, Inc. Publishers, 1994.
McMillian, Elizabeth Jean, Ph.D. and Matt Gainer. *California Colonial: The Spanish and Rancho Revival Styles*. Atglen, Pennsylvania: Schiffer Publishing, Ltd., 2002.
McMillian, Elizabeth Jean and Melba Levick. *Casa California: Spanish Style Houses from Santa Barbara to San Clemente*. New York: Rizzoli Publishing International, 1996.
Michael, A.C. *An Artist in Spain*. London: Hodder & Stoughton.
Mizner, Addison and Alice A. *DeLamar. Florida Architecture of Addison* Mizner. New York: William Helburn Inc., 1928. Reprinted by Dover Publications in 1992 with a new introduction by Donald W. Curl.
Mizner, Addison. *The Many Mizners*. New York: Sears Publishing Co., 1932.
Modern Homes: *Their Design and Construction*. Chicago: American Builder Publishing Corporation, 1931.
Moncanut, V. Casellas. *Arte y Decoracion en España*. 10 vols. Barcelona, Spain: J.M. Fabre, 1917–1924.
Moore, Charles, Gerald Allen and Donlyn Lyndon. *The Place of Houses*. New York: Holt, Rinehart and Winston, 1974.
Moore, Charles, Peter Becker and Regula Campbell. *The City Observed: A Guide to its Architecture and Landscapes*. New York: Vintage Books, 1984.
Myrick, David F. Montecito and Santa Barbara. Vol. 1: From Farms to Estates. Vol. II: *The Days of the Great Estates*. Glendale, California: Trans–Anglo Books, 1988 and 1991.
Neff, Wallace. *Architecture of Southern California: A Selection of Photographs, Plans and Scale Details from the Work of Wallace Neff*, FAIA. Chicago: Rand McNally, 1964.
Neff, Wallace, Jr., ed., and Alson Clark. Wallace Neff: *Architect of California's Golden Age*. Santa Barbara, California: Capra Press, 1986.
Newcomb, Rexford. *The Spanish House for America*. Philadelphia: J.B. Lippincott Company, 1927.
——. *Mediterranean Domestic Architecture in the United States*. leveland, Ohio: J.H. Jansen, 1928. Reprinted in 1999 by Acanthus Books with a new introduction by Marc Appleton.
——. *Spanish Colonial Architecture in the United States*. New York: J.J. Augustin Publisher, 1937.
Nichols, Rose Standish. *Spanish and Portuguese Gardens*. Boston: Houghton Mifflin Company, 1924.
Orr, Christina. *Addison Mizner: Architect of Dreams and Realities (1872–1933)*. West Palm Beach: Davies Publishing Co., 1932.
Ovnick, Merry and Carol Monteverde. *Los Angeles: The End of the Rainbow*. Los Angeles: Balcony Press, 1994.
Padilla, Victoria. *Southern California Gardens*. Berkeley, California: University of California Press, 1961.
Patterson, Augusta Owen. *American Homes of To–Day: Their Architectural Style, Their Environment, Their Characteristics*. New York: MacMillan Co., 1924.

Polley, G.H. *Spanish Architecture and Ornament*. Boston: Geo. H. Polley & Co., 1889.

Polyzoides, Stefanos, Roger Sherwood, James Tice, Julius Shulman. *Courtyard Housing in Los Angeles*. Berkeley, California: University of California Press, 1982.

Power, Nancy Goslee. *The Gardens of California: Four Centuries of Design from Mission to Modern*. New York: Clarkson Potter/Publishers, 1995.

Peixotto, Ernest. *Romantic California*. New York: Scribner's, 1917.

Prentice, A.N. *Renaissance Architecture and Ornament in Spain*. London: B.T. Batsford, 1888.

Requa, Richard S. *Architectural Details: Spain and the Mediterranean*. Cleveland, Ohio: J.H. Jansen, 1927.

——. *Old World Inspiration for American Architecture*. Los Angeles, California: The Monolith Portland Cement Company, 1929.

Roy A. Hilton Company. *Spanish Houses of California*. Long Beach: 1925.

Saylor, Henry H. "The Mediterranean Influence." *Garden and Home Builder* 44 (November 1926): 207.

Schneider, Mike. *California Potteries: The Complete Book*. Atglen, Pennsylvania: Schiffer Publising, Ltd., 1984.

Sexton, R.W. *Spanish Influence on American Architecture and Decoration*. New York: Brentano's, 1926.

Soule, Winsor. *Spanish Farm Houses and Minor Public Buildings*. New York: Architectural Book Publishing Co., 1924.

Staats, H. Philip. *California Architecture in Santa Barbara*. New York: Architectural Book Publishing Company, Inc., 1929. Reprinted in 1990 with a new introduction by David Gebhard.

Stanton, J.E. *By Middle Seas*. Los Angeles: Gladding McBean & Co, 1927.

Starr, Kevin. *Americans and the California Dream, 1850–1915*. New York: Oxford University Press, 1973.

——. *Inventing the Dream: California Through the Progressive Era*. New York: Oxford University Press, 1985.

——. *Material Dreams: Southern California Through the 1920s*. New York: Oxford University Press, 1990.

Starr, Kevin. *Material Dreams: Southern California Through the 1920s*. New York: Oxford University Press, 1990.

Streatfield, David C. *California Gardens: Creating a New Eden*. New York: Abbeville Press Publishers, 1994.

Streatfield, David C. *Historical Narrative: The Gardens of Rancho Los Alamitos*. Rancho Los Alamitos Foundation, 1987, updated 1994.

——. "The Garden at Casa del Herrero." *Antiques* 130 (August 1986): 287–88.

——. "The Evolution of the California Landscape." *Landscape Architecture*. Part 1. "Settling into Arcadia" (January 1976): 39–46.

——. "The Evolution of the California Landscape." *Landscape Architecture*. Part 2. "Arcadia Compromised" (March 1976): 117–26.

——. "The Evolution of the California Landscape." *Landscape Architecture*. Part 3. "The Great Promotions" (May 1977): 229–49.

——. "The Evolution of the California Landscape." *Landscape Architecture*. Part 4. "Suburbia at the Zenith" (September 1977): 417–24.

Taylor, Benjamin R. *George Owen Knapp: A Splendid Secret*. California: Benjamin R. Taylor, 2004.

Tilman, Jeffrey T. *Arthur Brown, Jr.: Progressive Classicist*. New York: W. W. Norton & Co., 2006.

Van Pelt, Garrett. *Old Architecture of Southern Mexico*. Cleveland, Ohio: J.H. Jansen, 1926.

Van Pelt, *John V. Masterpieces of Spanish Architecture: Romanesque and Allied Styles*. New York: Pencil Points Press, 1925.

Vogt, Elizabeth E. *Montecito: California's Garden Paradise*. Santa Barbara, California: MIP Publishing, 1993.

Waters, George. "Lotusland." *Pacific Horticulture* 44 (Spring 1983): 20–25.

Whitaker, Charles Harris, ed. *Bertram Grosvenor Goodhue: Architect and Master of Many Arts*. New York: Press of the American Institute of Architects, 1925.

Whittlesey, Austin. *The Minor Ecclesiastical, Domestic and Garden Architecture of Southern Spain*. New York: Architectural Book Publishing Co., 1917.

——. *The Renaissance Architecture of Central and Northern Spain*. New York: Architectural Book Publishing Co., 1920.

Winslow, Carleton Monroe, Bertram Grosvenor Goodhue and Clarence S. Stein . *The Architecture and the Gardens of the San Diego* Exposition. San Francisco: Paul Elder and Company, 1916.

Winslow, Carleton Monroe and Edward Fisher Brown, eds. *Small House Design*. 3rd. ed. Santa Barbara, California: Community Arts Association of Santa Barbara,California, 1924.

Woodbridge, Sally. *Historical Narrative: An Architectural History of Rancho Los Alamitos*. Rancho Los Alamitos Foundation. [No Date]

Wright, Richardson Little. *House and Garden: Second Book of Houses*. New York: Condé Nast Publishers, Inc., 1925.

Yerbury, F.R. *Lesser Known Architecture of Spain*. New York: William Helburn Inc., 1925.

Yoch, James J. *Landscaping the American Dream: The Gardens and Film Sets of Florence Yoch: 1890–1972*. New York: Harry N. Abrams, 1989.

ACKNOWLEDGMENTS

First and foremost, we wish to thank the current owners and residents, and in some cases the foundations, who allowed us to photograph and include their properties in this book. They are the current stewards of California's rich Mediterranean architectural heritage without whose commitment and care it might easily be lost. We would also like to thank the original owners, as well as all the architects, landscape architects, designers, and contractors, deceased or living, who originally crafted these houses and gardens or have restored and embellished them over time. Their appreciation of the Mediterranean Revival tradition is a testament to its enduring appeal. The names of all the above people would comprise too long a list here, but they appear more appropriately within the book's chapters.

Additional thanks go to a number of individuals who generously lent their time and advice in our efforts to obtain information and locate potential properties that might best represent different architectural examples. They are: Bob Attiyeh, Patrick Aumont, Sydney Baumgartner, Bob Burchman, Diane Galt, Kirk Gradin, Lana Hale, Virginia Hall, Stephen Harby, Buzz Hays, Julie Heinsheimer, Lynette Hernandez, Judy Horton, Debra Knowles, Michael Manheim, Deborah Miller, David Mossler, Liz Moule, Max Pierce, Ed Pinson, Stefanos Polyzoides, Tom Proctor, Alexandra Rasic, Suzanne Rheinstein, Kathleen Riquelme, Pamela Seager, Patti Skouras, Paul Spitzzeri, Pam Waterman, and Hutton Wilkinson.

We would also like to thank A & I Color Lab for their excellent work in processing our film. Domiane Forte was of great help in his comments on the manuscript, as were Kelly Thompson and Keegan Xavi in assisting with coordination of the materials for the book. Thanks are due to DeAnne Millais for her patient and devoted administrative support throughout, as well as to our designer Abigail Sturges, who pulled it all together and gave the book its final shape. Finally, this book would not have been possible without the guidance, wisdom, and support of our editors, Diana Lind, Douglas Curran, and most especially, David Morton, who has been our chief shepherd from the start. — M.A. and M.L.

INDEX